50 Philosophy Ideas
You Really
Need to Know

Ben Dupré

T0016608

greenfinch

Contents

Introduction

For most of its long history philosophy has had more than its share of dangerous people armed with dangerous ideas. On the strength of their supposedly subversive ideas, Descartes, Spinoza, Hume and Rousseau, to name but a few, were variously threatened with excommunication, obliged to postpone publication of their works, denied professional preferment, or forced into exile. And most notorious of all, the Athenian state regarded Socrates as so baneful an influence that they executed him. Not many of today's philosophers are executed for their beliefs, which is a pity – to the extent, at least, that it is a measure of how much the sense of danger has ebbed away.

Philosophy is now seen as the archetypal academic discipline, its practitioners firmly closeted in their ivory towers, detached from the problems of real life. The caricature is in many ways far from the truth. The questions of philosophy may be invariably profound and often difficult, but they also matter. Science, for instance, has the potential to fill the toyshop with all sorts of wonderful toys, from designer babies to GM foods, but unfortunately it has not provided – and cannot provide – the instruction book. To decide what we should do, rather than what we can do, we must turn to philosophy. Sometimes philosophers get swept along by the sheer delight of hearing their own brains turning over (and it can indeed make entertaining listening), but more often they bring clarity and understanding to questions that we should all care about. It is precisely these questions that this book aims to pick out and explore.

It is customary for authors to heap most of the credit on others and to reserve most of the blame for themselves; customary, perhaps, but strangely illogical (since the two should surely stick together), so hardly commendable in a book on philosophy. In the spirit of P.G. Wodehouse, therefore, who dedicated *The Heart of a Goof* to his daughter, 'without whose never-failing sympathy and encouragement [the] book would have been finished in half the time', I gladly apportion at least some of the credit to others. In particular, I would also like to thank my publisher at Quercus, Richard Milbank, for his unflagging support. And thanks, also, to my wife, Geraldine, and children, Sophie and Lydia.

01 The brain in a vat

Imagine that a human being has been subjected to an operation by an evil scientist. The person's brain has been removed from the body and placed in a vat of nutrients that keep the brain alive. The nerve endings have been connected to a super-scientific computer that causes the person to have the illusion that everything is perfectly normal. There seem to be people, objects, the sky, etc.; but really all the person is experiencing is the result of electronic impulses travelling from the computer to the nerve endings.

A nightmare scenario, the stuff of science-fiction? Perhaps, but of course that's exactly what you would say if you were a brain in a vat! Your brain may be in a vat rather than a skull, but your every experience is exactly as it would have been if you were living as a real body in a real world. The world around you – your chair, the book in your hands, your hands themselves – are all part of the illusion, thoughts and sensations fed into your disembodied brain by the scientist's super-powerful computer.

You probably don't believe you are a brain floating in a vat. Most philosophers probably don't believe they're brains in vats. But you don't have to believe it, you only have to admit you can't be certain that you're not. The problem is that, if you do happen to be a brain in a vat, all the things you think you know about the world will be false. And if that's *possible* you don't really know anything at all. The mere possibility appears to undermine our claims to knowledge about the external world. So is there any escape from the vat?

Vat origins

The classic modern telling of the brain-in-a-vat story above was given by the American philosopher Hilary Putnam in his 1981 book *Reason, Truth, and History*, but the germ of the idea has a much longer history. Putnam's thought experiment is essentially an updated version of a 17th-century horror story – the evil demon (*malin génie*) conjured up by the French philosopher René Descartes in his 1641 *Meditations on First Philosophy*.

Descartes's aim was to reconstruct the edifice of human knowledge on unshakeable foundations, for which he adopted his 'method of doubt', – he discarded any beliefs susceptible to the slightest degree of uncertainty. After pointing out the unreliability of our senses and the confusion created by dreams, Descartes pushed his method of doubt to the limit:

'I shall suppose ... that some malicious demon of the utmost power and cunning has employed all his energies in order to deceive me. I shall think that the sky, the air, the earth, colours, shapes, sounds and all external things are merely the delusions of dreams which he has devised to ensnare my judgment.'

Amongst the debris of his former beliefs and opinions, Descartes espies a single speck of certainty – the *cogito* – on the (apparently) sure foundation of which he begins his task of reconstruction (see page 16).

Unfortunately for Putnam and Descartes, although both are playing devil's advocate – adopting sceptical positions in order to confound scepticism – many philosophers have been more impressed by their skill in setting the sceptical trap than by their subsequent attempts to extricate themselves from it. Appealing to his own causal theory of meaning, Putnam attempts to show that the brain-in-a-vat scenario is incoherent, but at most he appears to show that a brain in a vat could not in fact express the thought that it was a brain in a vat. In effect, he demonstrates that the state of being an envatted brain is invisible and indescribable from within, but it is unclear that this semantic victory (if such it is) goes far to address the problem in relation to knowledge.

Scepticism

The term 'sceptic' is commonly applied to people who are inclined to doubt accepted beliefs or who habitually mistrust people or ideas in general. In this sense scepticism can characterized as a healthy and open-minded tendency to test and probe popularly held beliefs. Such

The simulation argument

Ordinary people may be tempted to dismiss the sceptic's nightmarish conclusions, but we should not be too hasty. Indeed, an ingenious argument recently devised by the philosopher Nick Bostrom suggests that it is highly probable that we are *already* living in a computer simulation! Just consider ...

In the future it is likely that our civilization will reach a level of technology such that it can create incredibly sophisticated computer simulations of human minds and of worlds for those minds to inhabit. Relatively tiny resources will be needed to sustain such simulated worlds – a single laptop of the future could be home to thousands or millions of simulated minds – so in all probability simulated minds will vastly outnumber biological ones. The experiences of both biological and simulated minds will be indistinguishable and both will of course think that they are not simulated, but the latter (who will make up the vast majority of minds) will in fact be mistaken. We naturally couch this argument in terms of hypotheticals about the future, but who is to say that this 'future' hasn't already happened – that such computer expertise has not already been attained and such minds already simulated? We of course suppose that we are not computer-simulated minds living in a simulated world, but that may be a tribute to the quality of the programming. Following the logic of Bostrom's argument, it is very likely that our supposition is wrong!

a state of mind is usually a useful safeguard against credulity but may sometimes tip over into a tendency to doubt everything, regardless of the justification for doing so. But whether good or bad, being sceptical in this popular sense is quite different from its philosophical usage.

The philosophical sceptic doesn't claim that we know nothing – not least because to do so would be obviously self-defeating (one thing we could not know is that we know nothing). Rather, the sceptic's position is to challenge our right to make claims to knowledge. We think we know lots of things, but how can we defend those claims? What grounds can we produce to justify any particular claim to knowledge? Our supposed knowledge of the world is based on perceptions gained via our senses, usually mediated by our use of reason. But are not such perceptions open to error? Can we ever be sure we're not hallucinating or dreaming, or that our memory isn't playing tricks? If the experience of dreaming is indistinguishable from our waking experience we can never be certain that something we think to be the case is in fact the case – that what we take to be true is in fact true. Such concerns, taken to an extreme, lead to evil demons and brains in vats ...

Epistemology is the area of philosophy concerned with knowledge: determining what we know and how we know it and identifying the conditions to be met for something to count as knowledge. Conceived as such, it can be seen as a response to the sceptic's challenge; its history as a series of attempts to defeat scepticism. Many feel that subsequent philosophers have been no more successful than Descartes in vanquishing scepticism. The concern that in the end there is no sure escape from the vat continues to cast a deep shadow over philosophy.

the condensed idea
Are you an envatted brain?

02 Plato's cave

I magine you have been imprisoned all your life in a dark cave. Your hands and feet are shackled and your head restrained so that you can only look at the wall straight in front of you. Behind you is a blazing fire, and between you and the fire a walkway on which your captors carry statues and all sorts of objects. The shadows cast on the wall by these objects are the only things you and your fellow prisoners have ever seen, all you have ever thought and talked about.

Probably the best known of the many images and analogies used by the Greek philosopher Plato, the Allegory of the Cave, appears in Book 7 of *Republic*, the monumental work in which he investigates the form of the ideal state and its ideal ruler – the philosopher king. Plato's justification for giving the reins of government to philosophers rests on a detailed study of truth and knowledge, and it is in this context that the Allegory of the Cave is used.

Plato's conception of knowledge and its objects is complex and many-layered, as becomes clear as the parable of the cave continues.

Now suppose that you are released from your shackles and free to walk around the cave. Dazzled at first by the fire, you will gradually come to see the situation of the cave properly and to understand the origin of the shadows that you previously took to be real. And finally you are allowed out of the cave and into the sunlit world outside, where you see the fullness of reality illuminated by the brightest object in the skies, the Sun.

Interpreting the cave

The interpretation of Plato's cave has been much debated, but the broad significance is clear enough. The cave represents 'the realm of becoming' – the visible world of our everyday experience, where everything is imperfect and constantly changing. The chained captives (ordinary people) live in a world of conjecture and illusion, while the former prisoner, free to roam within the cave, attains the most accurate view of reality possible within the ever-changing world of perception and experience. By contrast, the world outside the cave represents 'the realm of being' – the intelligible world of truth populated by the objects of knowledge, which are perfect, eternal and unchanging.

The theory of Forms

In Plato's view, what is known must not only be true but also perfect and unchanging. However, nothing in the empirical world (represented by life within the cave) fits this description: a tall person is short next to a tree; an apple that appears red at noon looks black at dusk; and so on. As nothing in the empirical world is an object of knowledge, Plato proposed that there must be another realm (the world outside the cave) of perfect and unchanging entities, which he called 'Forms' (or Ideas). So, for instance, it is by virtue of imitating or copying the Form of Justice that all particular just actions are just. As is suggested in the Allegory of the Cave, there is a hierarchy among the Forms, and overarching them all is the Form of the Good (represented by the Sun), which gives the others their ultimate meaning and even underlies their existence.

The problem of universals

Plato's theory of Forms and the metaphysical basis that supports it may seem exotic and overelaborate, but the problem that it seeks to address – the so-called 'problem of universals' – has been a dominant theme in philosophy, in some guise or other, ever since. In the Middle Ages the philosophical battle lines were drawn up between the realists (or Platonists) on one side, who believed that universals such as redness and tallness existed independently of particular red and tall things; and the nominalists on the other, who held that they were mere names or labels that were attached to objects to highlight particular similarities between them.

Platonic love

The idea with which Plato is most commonly associated today – so-called Platonic love – flows naturally from the sharp contrast made in the Allegory of the Cave between the world of the intellect and the world of the senses. The classic statement of the idea that the most perfect kind of love is expressed not physically but intellectually appears in another famous dialogue, *Symposium*.

The same basic distinction, usually expressed in terms of realism and anti-realism, still resonates throughout many areas of modern philosophy. So a realist position holds that there are entities 'out there' in the world – physical things or ethical facts or mathematical properties – that exist independently of our knowing or experiencing them. Opposed to this kind of view, other philosophers, known as anti-realists, put forward proposals in which there is a necessary and internal link or relation between what is known and our knowledge of it. The basic terms of all such debates were set up more than 2,000 years ago by Plato, one of the first and most thoroughgoing of all philosophical realists.

In defence of Socrates

In his Allegory of the Cave Plato sets out to do more than illuminate his distinctive views on reality and our knowledge of it. This becomes clear in the final part of the story. Having ascended to the outside world and recognized the nature of ultimate truth and reality, the released prisoner is anxious to re-enter the cave and disabuse his benighted former companions. But accustomed now to the bright light of the world outside, at first he stumbles in the darkness of the cave and is considered a fool by those who are still held captive. They think that his journey has ruined him; they don't want to listen to him and may even try to kill him if he persists. In this passage Plato is alluding to the usual plight of the philosopher – ridicule and rejection – in attempting to enlighten ordinary people and to set them on the path to knowledge and wisdom. And in particular he is thinking of the fate of his teacher, Socrates (his mouthpiece in *Republic* as in most of his other dialogues), who refused throughout his life to temper his philosophical teachings and was finally, in 399 BC, executed by the Athenian state.

**the condensed idea
Earthly knowledge
is but shadow**

The veil of perception

How do we see (and hear and smell) the world? Most of us uncritically suppose that physical objects around us are more or less as we perceive them to be, but there are problems with this commonsensical notion that have led many philosophers to question whether we do in fact observe the outside world directly. In their view we only have direct access to inner 'ideas', 'impressions' or (in modern terms) 'sense data'. The 17th-century English philosopher John Locke used a celebrated image to elucidate this. Human understanding, he suggested, is like 'a closet wholly shut from light, with only some little openings left, to let in external visible resemblances, or ideas of things without'.

But there is a big snag with Locke's conception. We may suppose that the ideas that enter the closet are more or less faithful representations of things outside it, but in the end it is a matter of inference that these inner representations correspond closely to external objects – or indeed to anything at all. Our ideas, which are all that we have direct access to, form an impenetrable 'veil of perception' between us and the outside world.

In his 1690 *Essay Concerning Human Understanding* Locke gave one of the fullest accounts of what are known as 'representational' models of perception. Any such model that involves intermediate ideas or sense data drives a wedge between us and the external world, and it is in the fissure so formed that scepticism about our claims to knowledge takes root. It is only by re-establishing a direct link between observer and external object that the veil can be torn and the sceptic vanquished. So, given that the model causes such problems, why adopt it in the first place?

Primary and secondary qualities

The unreliability of our perceptions forms an important part of the sceptic's weaponry in attacking our claims to knowledge. The fact that a tomato can look anything from red to black depending on the lighting conditions is used by the sceptic to cast general doubt over our senses as a reliable pathway to knowledge. Locke hoped that a perceptual model in which inner ideas and outer objects were separated would disarm the sceptic. His argument depended crucially on a further distinction – between primary and secondary qualities.

The redness of a tomato is not a property of the tomato itself but a product of the interaction of various factors, including certain physical attributes of the tomato such as its texture and surface structure; the peculiarities of our own sensory system; and the environmental conditions prevailing at the time of the observation. These properties (or rather non-properties) do not belong to the tomato as such and are said to be 'secondary qualities'.

At the same time, a tomato has certain true properties, such as its shape, which do not depend on the conditions under which observed or indeed on the existence of an observer at all. These are its 'primary qualities', which explain and give rise to our experience of the secondary qualities. Unlike our ideas of secondary qualities, those of primary qualities (Locke thought) closely resemble the physical objects themselves and can afford knowledge of those objects. For this reason it is with primary qualities that science is largely concerned,

Today Berkeley's immaterialist theory is seen as a virtuosic if eccentric metaphysical tour de force. Ironically, though, Berkeley regarded *himself* as the great champion of common sense. Having deftly exposed the pitfalls in Locke's mechanistic conception of the world, he proposed a solution that seemed obvious to him and which dismissed all the dangers at a stroke, banishing both sceptical and atheistic concerns. It would be even more galling for Berkeley that his place in the popular imagination today is limited to Samuel Johnson's famous though uncomprehending rebuttal of immaterialism, recorded in Boswell's *The Life of Samuel Johnson*: 'Striking his foot with mighty force against a large stone, [he exclaimed] "I refute it *thus*."'

and crucially, with respect to the sceptical challenge, it is our ideas of primary qualities that are proof against the sceptic's doubts.

Stuck in Locke's closet

One of Locke's earliest critics was his Irish contemporary, George Berkeley. Berkeley accepted the representational model of perception in which the immediate objects of perception were ideas, but he recognized at once that far from defeating the sceptics, Locke's conception risked surrendering all to them. Holed up in his closet, Locke would never be in a position to check whether his supposed 'resemblances, or ideas of things without' actually resembled the external things themselves. He would never be able to lift the veil and look on the other side, so he was trapped in a world of representations and the sceptic's case was made.

Having lucidly set out the dangers of Locke's position, Berkeley came to an extraordinary conclusion. Rather than tear through the veil in an attempt to reconnect us with the external world, he concluded instead that there was nothing behind the veil to reconnect with! For Berkeley, reality consists in the 'ideas' or sensations themselves. With these, of course, we are already fully and properly connected, so the dangers of scepticism are evaded, but at quite a price – the denial of an external, physical world!

According to Berkeley's idealist (or immaterialist) theory, 'to exist is to be perceived' (*esse est percipi*). And so do things cease to exist the moment we stop looking at them? Berkeley accepts this consequence, but help is at hand – God. Everything in the universe is conceived all the time in the mind of God, so the existence and continuance of the (non-material) world is assured.

the condensed idea
What lies beyond the veil?

04 **Cogito ergo sum**

S tripped of every belief that could conceivably be doubted, adrift in a sea of seemingly bottomless uncertainty, Descartes desperately casts about for some foothold – some firm ground on which to rebuild the edifice of human knowledge …

'I noticed that while I was trying to think everything false, it was necessary that I, who was thinking this, was something. And observing that this truth, "I am thinking, therefore I exist" [*cogito ergo sum*], was so firm and sure that all the most extravagant suppositions of the sceptics were incapable of shaking it, I decided that I could accept it without scruple as the first principle of the philosophy I was seeking.' And so came the Frenchman René Descartes to think what is certainly the most famous and probably the most influential thought in the history of Western philosophy.

The method of doubt

Descartes was himself at the vanguard of the scientific revolution sweeping through Europe in the 17th century, and it was his ambitious plan to cast aside the tired dogmas of the medieval world and to 'establish the sciences' on the firmest of foundations. To this end he adopted his rigorous 'method of doubt'. Not content to pick out the odd rotten apple (to use his own metaphor), he empties the barrel

---

Language matters

The well-known Latin form – *cogito ergo sum* – is found in Descartes's *Principles of Philosophy* (1644), but in his *Discourse on the Method* (1637) the French version occurs (*je pense, donc je suis*) and in his most important work, *Meditations*, it does not appear in its canonical form at all. The traditional English translation – 'I think, therefore I am' – is unhelpful in that the force of the argument is only brought out by the continuous form of the present tense, so in philosophical contexts it is often rendered 'I am thinking, therefore I exist.'

Cogito ergo sum may be the best known of all philosophical sayings, but its precise origins are not entirely clear. Although it is inextricably linked to Descartes, the idea behind the *cogito* goes back well before his time. At the beginning of the fifth century AD, for instance, St Augustine wrote that we can doubt anything but the soul's own doubting, and the idea did not originate with him.

completely, discarding any belief that is open to the slightest degree of doubt. In a final twist, he imagines an evil demon intent only on deceiving him, so that even the apparently self-evident truths of geometry and mathematics are no longer certain.

It is at this point – stripped of everything, even his own body and senses, other people, the entire world outside him – that Descartes finds salvation in the *cogito*. However deluded he may be, however determined the demon to deceive him, there has to be someone or something to be deluded, someone or something to be deceived. Even if he is mistaken about everything else, he cannot doubt that he is there, at that moment, to think the thought that he may be thus mistaken. The demon 'will never bring it about that I am nothing so long as I think that I am something … *I am, I exist*, is necessarily true whenever it is put forward by me or conceived in my mind.'

The limits of the *cogito*

An early criticism of Descartes, taken up by many since, is that he infers too much from the *cogito* – that he is only entitled to the conclusion that there is thinking going on, not that it is he that is doing the thinking. But even if we concede that thoughts do indeed presuppose thinkers, it must be admitted that what Descartes's insight establishes is very limited. First, the *cogito* is essentially first-personal – my *cogito* only works for me, yours only for you: it is certainly not beyond the demon's powers to fool me into thinking that you are thinking (and therefore that you exist). Second, the *cogito* is essentially present tense: it is perfectly compatible with it that I cease to exist when I am not thinking. Third, the 'I' whose existence is established is extremely attenuated and elusive: I may have none of the biography and other attributes that I believe make me me, and indeed I may still be completely in the clutches of the deceiving demon.

In sum, the 'I' of the *cogito* is a bare instant of self-consciousness, a mere pinprick cut off from everything else, including its own past. So what can Descartes establish on so precarious a foundation?

Reconstructing knowledge

Descartes may have dug down to bedrock, but has he left himself any materials to start rebuilding? He seems to have set the bar impossibly high – nothing less than demon-proof certainty will do. As it turns out, the return journey is surprisingly (perhaps alarmingly) rapid. There are two main supports to Descartes's theory of knowledge. First he notes that a distinctive feature of the *cogito* is the clarity with which we can see that it must be so, and from this he concludes that there is a general rule '*that the things we conceive very clearly and very distinctly are all true*'. And how can we be sure of this? Because the clearest and most distinct idea of all is our idea of a perfect, all-powerful, all-knowing God.

God is the source of all our ideas, and since he is good, he will not deceive us; the use of our powers of observation and reason (which also come from God) will accordingly lead us to truth, not falsehood. With the arrival of God, the seas of doubt very quickly recede – the world is restored and the task of reconstructing our knowledge on a sound, scientific basis can begin.

Lingering doubts

Very few have been convinced by Descartes's attempt to climb out of the sceptical hole that he had dug for himself. Much attention has focused on the infamous 'Cartesian circle' – the apparent use of clear and distinct ideas to prove the existence of God, whose goodness then warrants our use of clear and distinct ideas. Whatever the force of this argument (and it is far from clear that Descartes in fact fell into so obvious a trap), it is hard to share his confidence that he has successfully exorcized the demon. Descartes cannot (and does not) deny the fact that deception does occur; and if we follow his general rule, that must mean that we can sometimes be mistaken in thinking that we have a clear and distinct idea of something. But obviously we cannot know that we are making such a mistake, and if we cannot identify such cases, the door is once again wide open to scepticism.

Descartes has been called the father of modern philosophy. He has a good claim to the title, but not quite for the reasons that he would have wished. His aim was to dispel sceptical doubts once and for all, so that we could confidently dedicate ourselves to the rational pursuit of knowledge, but in the end he was much more successful at raising such doubts than quelling them. Subsequent generations of philosophers have been transfixed by the issue of scepticism, which has been at or near the top of the philosophical agenda from the day that Descartes put it there.

the condensed idea
I am thinking therefore I exist

Reason and experience

How do we come to know things? Is it primarily through our use of reason that we acquire knowledge? Or does experience gained through our senses play the most significant role in the way we get to know the world? Much of the history of Western philosophy has been coloured by this basic opposition between reason and experience as the foundational principle of knowledge. Specifically, it is the main bone of contention between two extremely influential philosophical strands – rationalism and empiricism.

To understand what is at issue between rationalist and empiricist theories of knowledge, it is useful to look at three key distinctions that are used by philosophers to elucidate the differences between them.

A priori vs a posteriori
Something is knowable a priori if it can be known without reference to experience – that is, without any empirical investigation of how things actually stand in the world; '2 + 2 = 4' is known a priori – you do not have to go out into the world to establish its truth. By contrast, if such investigation is needed, something is only knowable a posteriori; so 'coal is black', if true, is an a posteriori truth – to verify it, you need to look at a lump of coal.

Analytic vs synthetic
A proposition is analytic if it does not give any more information than is already contained in the meanings of the terms involved. The truth of the statement 'All spinsters are unmarried' is apparent merely by virtue of understanding the meaning and relation of the words used. By contrast, the statement 'All spinsters are miserable' is synthetic – it brings together (synthesizes) different concepts and so provides significant information (or misinformation). To establish whether it is true or not, you would have to enquire into the mental state of every unmarried woman.

Necessary vs contingent
A necessary truth is one that could not be otherwise – it must be true in any circumstances, or in all possible worlds. A contingent truth is true but might not have been if things in the world had been different.

For instance, the statement 'Most boys are naughty' is contingent –
it may or may not be true. By contrast, if it is true that all boys are
naughty and that Ludwig is a boy, it is necessarily true (in this case, as
a matter of logic) that Ludwig is naughty.

There seems to be an obvious alignment between these distinctions:
so, on the face of it, an analytic statement, if true, is necessarily so and
is known a priori; and a synthetic proposition, if true, is contingently
so and is known a posteriori. In fact, however, things are not nearly so
neat, and the chief difference between empiricists and rationalists can
be captured by the different way they choose to line up these terms.
Thus the task of rationalists is to show that there are synthetic a priori
statements – that significant or meaningful facts about the world can
be discovered by rational, non-empirical means. Conversely, the aim
of the empiricist is often to show that apparently a priori facts, such as
those of mathematics, are in fact analytic (see box on page 22).

Alternatives to foundationalism

Rationalists and empiricists may differ on many things, but they do
at least agree that there is *some* basis (reason or experience) on which
our knowledge is founded. So, for instance, the 18th-century Scottish

Kantian concerns

The analytic/synthetic distinction has its origins in the work of the
German philosopher Immanuel Kant. One of his main objectives
in the *Critique of Pure Reason* is to demonstrate that there are
certain concepts or categories of thought, such as substance and
causation, that we cannot learn from the world but that we are
required to use in order to make sense of it. Kant's main theme is
the nature and justification of these concepts and of the synthetic a
priori knowledge that stems from them.

Battleground mathematics

In the conflict between empiricism and rationalism, the field of mathematics has been the battleground on which the most intense fighting has taken place. For the rationalist, mathematics has always appeared to offer a paradigm of knowledge, presenting a realm of abstract objects about which discoveries could be made by the exercise of reason alone. An empiricist cannot let this go unchallenged, so is obliged either to deny that mathematical facts can be known in this way, or to show that such facts are essentially analytic or trivial. The latter course usually takes the form of arguing that the supposedly abstract facts of mathematics are actually human constructs and that mathematical thinking is at root a matter of convention: in the end there is consensus, not discovery; proof, not truth.

philosopher David Hume may criticize Descartes for his chimerical search for a rock of rational certainty from which he could corroborate all our knowledge, including the truthfulness of our senses. But Hume does not deny that there is *any* basis, merely that this foundation can exclude our common experience and natural systems of belief.

So both rationalism and empiricism are essentially foundationalist, but there are other approaches that dispense with this basic assumption. An influential alternative is coherentism, in which knowledge is seen as an interlocking mesh of beliefs, all the strands of which support each other to form a coherent body or structure. But it is, though, a structure without a single foundation, hence the coherentist slogan: 'every argument needs premises, but there is nothing that is the premise of every argument.'

Historically, the British empiricists of the 17th and 18th centuries – Locke, Berkeley and Hume – are often ranged against their Continental 'rivals', the rationalists Descartes, Leibniz and Spinoza. But as usual, such easy categorizations obscure much of the detail. The archetype on one side, Descartes, often shows himself to be sympathetic to empirical inquiry, while Locke, the archetype on the other, sometimes appears willing to grant the space that rationalists would give to some form of intellectual insight or intuition.

the condensed idea
How do we know?

06 The tripartite theory of knowledge

'**U**h oh, wrong turn,' thought Don, as he saw the hated figure slumped against the lamp-post, the all-too-familiar features of his brutish face clearly visible in the yellow light. 'I should have known that that scum would surface here. Well, now I know … What are you waiting for, Eric? If you're so tough… ' All his attention focused on the figure in front of him, Don didn't hear the footsteps approaching from behind. And he didn't feel a thing as Eric delivered the fatal blow to the back of his head…

So did Don really know that his killer Eric was there in the alley that night? Don certainly believed that he was there in front of him, and his belief proved to be correct. And he had every reason to form such a belief: he had no idea that Eric had an identical twin called Alec, and he had a clear view of a man who was indistinguishable from Eric in every respect.

Plato's definition of knowledge

Our intuition is that Don did not in fact know that Eric was present in the alley – in spite of the fact that Eric was indeed there, Don believed that he was there, and he was apparently perfectly justified in forming that belief. But in saying this, we are running counter to one of the most hallowed definitions in the history of philosophy.

In his dialogue *Theaetetus* Plato conducts a masterful investigation into the concept of knowledge. The conclusion he reaches is that knowledge is 'true belief with a *logos*' (that is, with a 'rational account' of why the belief is true), or simply, 'justified true belief'. This so-called tripartite theory of knowledge can be expressed more formally as follows:

A person S knows proposition P if and only if:
1. P is true
2. S believes P
3. S is justified in believing P

According to this definition, (1), (2) and (3) are the necessary and sufficient conditions for knowledge. Conditions (1) and (2) have generally been accepted without much debate – you cannot know a falsehood and you have to believe what you claim to know. And few have questioned the need for some form of appropriate justification, as stipulated by (3): if you believe that Noggin will win the Kentucky Derby as a result of sticking a pin in a list of runners and riders, you will not generally be held to have known it, even if Noggin happens to be first past the post. You just got lucky.

Gettier's spanner in the works

Much attention was predictably given to the precise form and degree of justification required by condition (3), but the basic framework provided by the tripartite theory was broadly accepted for nearly 2,500 years. Then, in 1963, a spanner was very adeptly put in the works by the US philosopher Edmund Gettier. In a short paper Gettier provided

The Comedy of Errors

The technique of using mistaken identity, especially identical twins, to question knowledge that is (apparently) justifiably held, is well known to anyone familiar with Shakespeare's plays. For instance, in *The Comedy of Errors* there are not one, but two, pairs of identical twins: Antipholus and Dromio of Syracuse and Antipholus and Dromio of Ephesus – separated at birth during a shipwreck. Shakespeare uses their coming together to create an ingenious farce that can be analysed in the same way as Gettier's counterexamples. So, when Antipholus of Syracuse arrives in Ephesus, Angelo, the local goldsmith, hails him 'Master Antipholus'. Confused, not having set foot in Ephesus before, Antipholus of Syracuse responds 'Ay, that's my name.' Angelo replies 'I know it well, sir'. In fact, Angelo *knows* nothing of the sort. According to the tripartite theory his belief is justified, yet it is pure coincidence that his customer has an identical twin of the same name.

counterexamples, similar in spirit to the tale of Don, Eric and Alec, in which someone formed a belief that was both true and justified – that is, met the three conditions stipulated by the tripartite theory – and yet apparently did not qualify as knowing what he thought he knew.

The problem exposed by Gettier-type examples is that in these cases the justification for holding a belief is not connected in the right sort of way to the truth of that belief, so that its truth is more or less a matter of luck. Much energy has since been spent on trying to plug the gap exposed by Gettier. Some philosophers have questioned the whole project of attempting to define knowledge in terms of necessary and sufficient conditions. More often, though, attempts to solve the Gettier problem have involved finding an elusive 'fourth condition' that can be bolted onto the Platonic model.

Many suggested improvements to the concept of justification have been 'externalist' in nature, focusing on factors that lie outside the

Should knowledge be indefeasible?

One suggestion for the fourth condition to supplement the tripartite theory is that knowledge should be what philosophers call 'indefeasible'. The idea is that there should be nothing that someone might have known that would have overridden the reasons they had for believing something. So, for instance, if Don had known that Eric had an identical twin brother, he would not have been justified in believing that the man leaning against the lamp-post was Eric. But by the same reasoning, if knowledge has to be indefeasible in this way, Don wouldn't have *known* that it was Eric *even if it had been*. This is the case whether or not Don knew of the twin brother's existence; there could always be some such factor, so there will always be a sense in which knowers never know that they know. Like many other responses to the Gettier problem, the demand for indefeasibility risks setting the bar so very high that little of what we usually count as knowledge will pass the test.

psychological states of the putative knower. For instance, a causal theory insists that the promotion of true belief to knowledge depends on the belief being caused by relevant external factors. It is because Don's belief is causally related to the wrong person – Alec, not Eric – that it does not count as knowledge.

Since Gettier's paper, the search for a 'patch' has developed into a sort of philosophical arms race. Attempted enhancements of the tripartite definition have been met with a barrage of counterexamples intended to show that some flaw is still there. Proposals that apparently avoid the Gettier problem tend to do so at the cost of excluding much of what we intuitively count as knowledge.

the condensed idea
When do we really know?

07 **The mind-body problem**

Since the 17th century the march of science has swept all before it. The route mapped out by Copernicus, Newton, Darwin and Einstein is dotted with numerous significant milestones along the way, giving hope that in time even the remotest regions of the universe and the innermost secrets of the atom will be exposed by science. Or will they? For there is one thing – at once the most obvious and most mysterious thing of all – that has so far resisted the best efforts of scientist and philosopher alike: the human mind.

We are all immediately conscious of our consciousness – that we have thoughts, feelings, desires that are subjective and private to us; that we are actors at the centre of our world and have a unique and personal perspective on it. In stark contrast, science is triumphantly objective, open to scrutiny, eschewing the personal and the perspectival. So how can something as strange as consciousness conceivably exist in the physical world that is being exposed by science? How are mental phenomena explicable in terms of, or otherwise related to, physical states and events in the body? These questions together form the mind–body problem, arguably the thorniest of all philosophical issues.

As in epistemology (the philosophy of knowledge), so in the philosophy of mind, the Frenchman René Descartes made an impact in the 17th century that has reverberated through Western philosophy until the present day. Descartes's refuge in the certainty of his own self (see page 16) naturally led him to give an exalted status to mind in relation to everything in the world outside it. In metaphysical terms, he conceived mind as an entirely distinct entity – as mental substance, whose essential nature is thinking. Everything else is matter, or material substance, whose defining characteristic is spatial extension (that is, filling physical space). Thus he envisaged two distinct realms, one of immaterial minds, with mental properties such as thinking and feeling; another of material bodies, with physical properties such as mass and shape. It was this picture of the relation between mind and matter, known as 'substance dualism', that Gilbert Ryle pilloried as the 'dogma of the Ghost in the Machine' (see box opposite).

Ryle's Ghost

In his book *The Concept of Mind* (1949) the English philosopher Gilbert Ryle argues that Descartes's dualist conception of mind and matter is based on a 'category mistake'. Imagine, for instance, a tourist who is shown all the separate colleges, libraries and other buildings that make up Oxford University, and then complains at the end of the tour that he hasn't seen the university. The tourist has wrongly ascribed both the university and the buildings of which it is composed to the same category of existence, thus entirely misrepresenting the relation between the two. In Ryle's view, Descartes has made a similar blunder in the case of mind and matter, mistakenly supposing them to be different substances. From this dualist metaphysics arises Ryle's disparaging picture of the 'Ghost in the Machine': the immaterial mind or soul (the Ghost) somehow living within and pulling the levers of the material body (the Machine). After delivering his withering attack on Cartesian dualism, Ryle goes on to present his own solution to the mind–body problem – behaviourism (see page 39).

Problems for dualism

A desire to drink causes my arm to lift the glass; a drawing pin in my foot causes me pain. Mind and body (so common sense suggests) interact: mental events bring about physical ones, and vice versa. But the need for such interaction immediately casts doubt on the Cartesian picture. It is a basic scientific principle that a physical effect requires a physical cause, but by making mind and matter *essentially* different, Descartes appears to have made interaction impossible.

Descartes himself recognized the problem and realized that it would take God's intervention to effect the necessary causal relationship, but he did little else to resolve the issue. Descartes's younger contemporary and follower, Nicolas Malebranche, accepted his dualism and took it upon himself to grapple with the causation problem. His surprising solution was to claim that interaction did not in fact occur at all. Instead, on every occasion when a conjunction of

Descartes may have made the classic statement of substance dualism, but he was by no means the first. Indeed, some form of dualism is implicit in any philosophy, religion or world-view that presupposes there is a supernatural realm in which immaterial bodies (souls, gods, demons, angels and the like) reside. The idea that a soul can survive the death of a physical body or be reincarnated in another body (human or other) also requires some kind of dualist conception of the world.

mental and physical events was required, God acted to make it happen, so creating the appearance of cause and effect. The awkwardness of this doctrine, known as 'occasionalism', has won little support and serves principally to highlight the seriousness of the problem it was intended to fix.

A tempting way to avoid some problems facing the Cartesian position is *property dualism*, originating in the work of Descartes's Dutch contemporary, Baruch Spinoza, who claims the notion of dualism relates not to substances but to properties: two distinct types of property, mental and physical, can be ascribed to a single thing (a person or subject), but these attributes are irreducibly different and cannot be analysed in terms of one another. So the different properties describe different *aspects* of the same entity (hence the view is sometimes called the 'double aspect theory'). The theory can explain how mind–body interaction occurs, as the causes of our actions themselves have both physical and mental aspects. But, in ascribing such essentially different properties to a single subject, there is a suspicion that property dualism has merely shifted the most daunting problem facing substance dualism, rather than solving it.

Physicalism

The obvious response to the difficulties facing the substance dualism of Descartes is to adopt a monistic approach – to claim that there is only one kind of 'stuff' in the world, either mental or physical, not two. A few, most notably George Berkeley (see page 14), have taken the idealist path, claiming that reality consists of nothing but minds and their ideas, but the great majority, certainly amongst today's philosophers, have opted for some form of physicalist explanation. Driven on by the undeniable successes of science in other areas, the physicalist insists that the mind, too, must be brought within the purview of science; and since the subject matter of science is exclusively physical, the mind must also be physical. The task then becomes to explain how mind (subjective and private) fits into a complete and purely physical account of the world (objective and publicly accessible).

Physicalism has taken a number of different forms, but what these have in common is that they are reductive: they claim to show that mental phenomena can be analysed, fully and exhaustively, in purely physical terms. Advances in neuroscience have left little doubt that mental states are intimately related to states of the brain. The simplest course for the physicalist is thus to claim that mental phenomena are actually identical to physical events and processes in the brain. The most radical versions of such identity theories are 'eliminative': they propose that, as our scientific understanding advances, 'folk psychology' – our ordinary ways of thinking and expressing our mental lives, in terms of beliefs, desires, intentions and so on – will disappear, to be replaced by accurate concepts and descriptions drawn principally from neuroscience.

Physicalist solutions to the mind–body problem brush aside many of the difficulties of dualism at a stroke. In particular, the mysteries of causation that torment dualists are dispelled by simply bringing consciousness within the scope of scientific explanation. Predictably, critics of physicalism complain that its proponents have brushed aside too much; that its successes have been achieved at the heaviest cost – of failing to capture the essence of conscious experience, its subjective nature.

the condensed idea
Mind boggles

08 What is it like to be a bat?

'**I**magine that one has webbing on one's arms, which enables one to fly around at dusk and dawn catching insects in one's mouth; that one has very poor vision, and perceives the surrounding world by a system of reflected high-frequency sound signals; and that one spends the day hanging upside down by one's feet in an attic. In so far as I can imagine this (which is not very far), it tells me only what it would be like for *me* to behave as a bat behaves. But that is not the question. I want to know what it is like for a *bat* to be a bat.'

In the philosophy of mind US philosopher Thomas Nagel's 1974 article 'What is it like to be a bat?' has probably been more influential than any other paper in recent times. Nagel succinctly captures the essence of the discontent that many feel with current attempts to analyse our mental life and consciousness in purely physical terms. As such his paper has almost become a totem for philosophers dissatisfied with such physicalist and reductive theories of mind.

The bat perspective

Nagel's central point is that there is a 'subjective character of experience' – something that it is to be a particular organism, some thing it is like *for* the organism – that is never captured in these reductive accounts. Take the case of a bat. Bats navigate and locate insects in complete darkness by a system of sonar, or echolocation, by emitting high-frequency squeaks and detecting their reflections as they bounce back from surrounding objects. This form of perception is completely unlike any sense that we possess, so it is reasonable to suppose that it is subjectively completely unlike anything we are able to experience. In effect, there are experiences that we as humans could never experience, even in principle; there are facts about experience whose exact nature is quite beyond our comprehension. The essential incomprehensibility of these facts is due to their subjective nature – to the fact that they essentially embody a particular point of view.

There is a tendency among physicalist philosophers to cite examples of successful scientific reduction, such as the analysis of water as H_2O or of lightning as an electrical discharge, and then to suggest that these cases are similar to the analysis of mental phenomena in terms of physical phenomena. Nagel denies this: the success of this kind of scientific analysis is based on moving towards greater objectivity by moving away from a subjective point of view; and it is precisely the omission of this subjective element from physicalist theories of the mind that makes them incomplete and unsatisfactory. As he concludes, 'it is a mystery how the true character of experiences could be revealed in the physical operation of that organism', which is all that science has to offer.

What Mary didn't know

Nagel is apparently content to leave the matter as a mystery – to highlight the failure of recent physicalist theories to capture the subjective element that seems to be essential to consciousness. He professes to be opposed to these reductive approaches, not to physicalism as such. The Australian philosopher Frank Jackson attempts to go further. In a much-discussed 1982 paper 'What Mary didn't know', he presents a thought experiment about a girl who knows every conceivable physical fact about colour. Now, if physicalism were true, Jackson argues, Mary would know all there is to know. But it turns out that there are things (facts) she doesn't know after all: she doesn't know what it is like to see colours; she learns what it is like to see red (etc.). Jackson concludes that there are facts that are not, and cannot be, captured by physical theory – non-physical facts – and hence that physicalism is false (see box on page 34).

Committed physicalists are not, of course, persuaded by Jackson's argument. Objections are levelled primarily at the status of his so-called 'non-physical facts': some critics accept that they are facts but deny that they are non-physical, others assert that they are not facts at all. The root of these objections is generally that Jackson has begged the question against physicalism: if physicalism is true and Mary knows all the physical facts that could ever be known about colour, then she will indeed know all there is to know about redness, including subjective experiences associated with it. There is also a suspicion of the masked man fallacy (see box on page 35) in the way Jackson uses Mary's psychological states to make the necessary distinction between physical and non-physical facts.

Monochrome Mary

From the moment of her birth Mary was confined in a black-and-white room, where she was never exposed to anything that was not black, white or shades of grey. Her education may have been unusual but was certainly not neglected, and by reading books (no colour books of course) and watching lectures on black-and-white television, she eventually became the world's greatest scientist. She learned literally everything there was to know (and could ever be known) about the physical nature of the world, about us and about our environment. Finally the day came when Mary was let out of her monochrome room and into the world outside. And what a shock she had! She saw colours for the first time. She learned what it was like to see red and blue and yellow. So, even though she knew every physical fact about colour, there were still things about colour that she didn't know...

Moral:
1. there are some facts that are not physical;
2. be very careful how you pick your parents.

Whatever the strength of the arguments against Mary, it is hard not to feel that both Jackson and Nagel have put their finger on *something* – that something essential is missing from the versions of physicalism that have been proposed to date. It is perhaps safe to conclude that the issue of accommodating consciousness in a purely physical account of the world still has plenty of life left in it.

The masked man

According to Leibniz's law or the 'identity of indiscernibles', if two things, A and B, are identical, every property of A will be a property of B; and hence, if A has a property that B lacks, A and B are not identical. Now Bertie thinks that Bono is the greatest rock star in the world, but he has no view about Paul Hewson (he doesn't realize that it is in fact Bono's original name). That means that Bono has a property that Paul Hewson lacks – the property of being thought by Bertie to be the greatest rock star in the world – so, according to Leibniz's law, Bono is not the same person as Paul Hewson. But he is, so something has gone wrong with the argument. The problem is due to the so-called masked man fallacy: I don't know who the masked man is; I know who my brother is; therefore my brother is not the masked man. The root of the fallacy is that subjective views or beliefs about something are not real properties of that thing: you can know something under different descriptions, just as different people can have different beliefs about the same thing.

Now, does Frank Jackson's thought experiment about Mary commit the masked man fallacy? Physicalist opponents have argued that he uses the 'wrong kind' of property to establish a duality of physical and non-physical facts. But in reality, they argue, there is only one kind of fact (physical facts) that can be given different, essentially subjective descriptions: two ways of looking at the same thing.

the condensed idea
Inside a bat's mind?

09 The Turing test

Parry:	*Cops arrest the wrong people.*
Interviewer:	*They arrest the right ones sometimes.*
Parry:	*The law should get those Italian crooks.*
Interviewer:	*Are you Italian?*
Parry:	*My background is British, but I was born in this country.*
Interviewer:	*Do you know any Italian crooks?*
Parry:	*I try to avoid the underworld.*
Interviewer:	*Are you afraid of the underworld?*
Parry:	*The mafia are the worst gangsters.*
Interviewer:	*Are you connected with the mafia?*
Parry:	*You know, they know me.*
Interviewer:	*How do they know you?*
Parry:	*They spy on me.*
Interviewer:	*Why do they?*
Parry:	*They want to get false evidence to frame me.*
Interviewer:	*What do they have against you?*
Parry:	*They are out to get me.*

Parry may sound like a man in trouble but, in fact, he's a computer program. Created in 1971 by Kenneth Colby, a psychiatrist at Stanford University, Parry was programmed to respond to questions in the manner of a schizophrenic with a paranoid fixation that he is a mafia target. Colby set up a test in which Parry was interviewed alongside a number of genuine paranoid patients and the results were then assessed by a panel of psychiatrists. No one on the panel guessed that Parry was not a real patient.

Can Parry think?

Twenty-one years before Parry's birth, in 1950, the British mathematician and computer pioneer Alan Turing wrote a seminal paper in which he proposed a test to determine whether a machine could think. The test, based on a party game called the imitation game, requires an interrogator to communicate with a human and a machine both physically separated from her, by some form of electronic link. She can ask any question in order to distinguish machine and the human, and if after a certain period of time she is unable to do so, the machine is said to have passed the test.

Did Parry pass the test? Not really. To count as a proper Turing test, the panel of psychiatrists (filling the role of the interrogator) should have been told that one of the patients was in fact a computer and that the task was to identify which. In any case Parry would very quickly have revealed itself if questioned more broadly. Turing himself believed that by the end of the 20th century advances in computer programming would have reached a point where an interrogator would have no more than a 70 percent chance of making a correct identification after five minutes of interviewing, but in fact progress has been far slower than he had anticipated. So far no computer program has come close to passing the Turing test.

Turing proposed his test to sidestep the question 'Can machines think?', which he regarded as too imprecise to be worth addressing, but the test is now widely accepted as the criterion by which to judge whether a computer program is able to think (or 'has a mind' or 'shows intelligence', according to taste). As such, it is seen as the benchmark by proponents (scientific and philosophical) of 'strong AI (artificial intelligence)' – the thesis that suitably programmed computers have minds (not just simulations of mind) in precisely the same sense as do humans.

The Chinese room

The most influential challenge to the Turing test has been posed by a thought experiment devised in 1980 by the US philosopher John Searle. He imagines himself – an English-speaker not knowing a word of Chinese – confined within a room into which batches of Chinese scripts are posted. He is already equipped with a pile of Chinese symbols and a copious rule book, in English, which explains how he is to post out certain combinations of symbols in response to strings of symbols in the batches posted to him. In time, he gets so adept at his task that, from the point of view of someone outside the room, his responses are indistinguishable from those of a native Chinese speaker. In other words, the inputs and outputs into and out of the room are exactly as they would be if he had a full understanding of Chinese. Yet all he is doing is manipulating uninterpreted formal symbols; he understands nothing.

Producing appropriate outputs in response to inputs, according to rules provided by a program (equivalent to Searle's English rule book), is precisely what a digital computer does. Like the incumbent of the Chinese room, Searle suggests, a computer program, however sophisticated, is no more than, and could never be more than, a mindless manipulator of symbols; it is essentially syntactic – it follows rules to manipulate symbols – but it can have no understanding of meaning, or semantics. Just as there is no understanding within the Chinese room, so there is none in a computer program: no understanding, no intelligence, no mind; and never more than a simulation of these things.

Passing the Turing test is basically a matter of providing appropriate outputs to given inputs, so the Chinese room, if accepted, undermines its claim to work as a test for a thinking machine. And if the Turing test goes, so too does the central thesis of strong AI. But these are not the only casualties. Two extremely significant approaches to the philosophy of mind are also undermined if the point of the Chinese room is granted.

Problems for behaviourism and functionalism

The central idea behind behaviourism is that mental phenomena can be translated, without any loss of content, into kinds of behaviour or dispositions to behaviour. So to say that someone is in pain, for example, is a sort of shorthand for saying that they are bleeding, grimacing, etc. In other words, mental events are defined entirely in terms of external, observable inputs and outputs, the sufficiency of which is explicitly denied by the Chinese room. Behaviourism, given its classic exposition by Gilbert Ryle (see page 29), had largely succumbed to a number of fatal objections before Searle's appearance. Its importance today is rather that it spawned a doctrine that is probably the most widely accepted theory of mind – functionalism.

Repairing many of the flaws in behaviourism, functionalism claims that mental states are functional states: a certain mental state is identified as such by virtue of the role or function it has in relation to various inputs (the causes that typically bring it about), the effects it has on other mental states, and various outputs (the effects it typically has on behaviour). To use a computer analogy, functionalism (like behaviourism) is a 'software solution' to the theory of mind: it defines mental phenomena in terms of inputs and outputs, with no consideration of the hardware platform (dualist, physicalist, whatever) on which the software is running. The problem, of course, is that focusing on inputs and outputs threatens to lead us straight back into the Chinese room.

the condensed idea
'Did you ever take that test yourself?'

10 The ship of Theseus

Boy, did Theo have problems with that car he bought at Joe's! It started off with little things – a door lock needed replacing, some fiddly bits in the rear suspension fell off, the usual. Then bigger stuff started to go wrong – first the clutch, then the gearbox, finally the whole transmission. And there were plenty of knocks along the way, so the car was rarely out of the body shop. And so it went on – and on and on... Unbelievable. 'But not as unbelievable,' Theo ruefully thought, 'as the fact that the car's just two years old and every single bit has now been replaced. Hey, look on the bright side – maybe I've got a new car!'

Is Theo right? Or is it still the same car? The tale of the car of Theo – or, more usually, the ship of Theseus – is one of many puzzles used by philosophers to test intuitions about the identity of things or persons over time. It seems our intuitions in this area are often strong but conflicting. The story of Theseus' ship was told by the English philosopher Thomas Hobbes, who then elaborated further. To pick up Theo's version...

Honest Joe didn't live up to his name. Most of the bits he'd replaced in Theo's car were working fine, and he'd mended any that weren't. He'd saved the old parts and had been fitting them together. After two years, he'd assembled an exact copy of Theo's car. He thought it was a copy. Maybe it was Theo's car?

Identity crises

Which is the original? The car Theo has, now built entirely of new parts, or Joe's version, built entirely of the original parts? It probably depends who you ask. Whichever, the identity of the car over time isn't nearly as neat and tidy as we might wish.

It isn't just a problem with cars and ships. People change enormously over a lifetime. Physically and psychologically, there may be very little in common between a 2-year-old toddler and the doddery 90-year-old who's taken his place 88 years later. So are they the same person? If they are, what makes them so? It matters – is it just to punish the 90-year-old for something he did 70 years earlier?

What if he doesn't remember it? Should a doctor allow the 90-year-old to die because that wish was expressed 40 years earlier by a (supposedly) previous version of himself?

This is the problem of personal identity, which has exercised philosophers for hundreds of years. So just what are the necessary and sufficient conditions for a person at one time being the same person at a later time?

Animals and brain transplants

The commonsense view is probably that personal identity is a matter of biology: I am now who I was in the past because I am the same living organism, the same human animal; I am linked to a particular body that is a single and continuous organic entity. But imagine for a moment a brain transplant – an operation we can envisage being within reach of future technology – in which *your* brain is transferred into my body. Our intuition is surely that *you* have a new body, not that my body has a new brain; if so, it seems that having a particular body is *not* a necessary condition of personal survival.

This consideration has led some philosophers to retreat from body to brain – to claim identity is linked not to the whole body but to the brain. This move fits our intuition regarding the brain transplant case but still does not quite do the job. Our concern is with what we suppose emanates from the brain, not with the physical organ itself. While we may be uncertain how brain activity gives rise to consciousness or mental activity, few doubt the brain somehow underlies that activity. In considering what makes me me, it is the 'software' of experiences, memories, beliefs, and so on, that concerns me, not the 'hardware' of a particular lump of grey matter. My sense of being me would not be much shaken if the total sum of those experiences, memories, and so on, were copied onto a synthetic brain, or indeed if someone else's brain could be reconfigured to hold all my memories, beliefs, and so on, I am my mind; I go where my mind goes. Based on this view, my identity isn't linked to my physical body, including my brain, at all.

Psychological continuity

Taking a psychological approach to the question of personal identity, rather than a biological or physical one, let's suppose that each part of my psychological history is joined to earlier parts by strands of enduring memories, beliefs, and so on. Not all (and perhaps none) of these need extend from start to finish; provided there is a single, overlapping lattice of such elements, then it remains my history. I remain me. The idea of psychological continuity as the main criterion of personal identity over time comes from John Locke. It is the dominant theory among contemporary philosophers, but is not without problems of its own.

Imagine, for instance, a *Star Trek*-style teleportation system. Suppose this records your physical composition down to the last atom and then transfers this data to some remote location (say from London, Earth, to Moonbase 1), where your body is exactly replicated (from new matter) at the precise moment your body in London is annihilated. All is well – provided you adhere to the psychological continuity thesis: there is an uninterrupted stream of memories, and so on, flowing from the individual in London to the one on the Moon, so psychological continuity and hence personal identity is preserved. You are in Moonbase 1. But suppose the transporter failed and neglected to carry out the annihilation in London. Now there are two of 'you' – one on Earth and one on the Moon. According to the continuity account, because the psychological stream is preserved in both cases, they are both you. In this case, we have little hesitation in saying that you are the individual in London while the one on the

Moon is a copy. But if this intuition is right, we seem to be forced back from the psychological to the biological/animal account: it appears to matter that you are the old meat in London rather than the new meat on the Moon.

Getting your self straight

Such mixed intuitions may come from asking the wrong questions, or applying the wrong concepts in answering them. David Hume drew attention to the elusiveness of the self, claiming that, however hard you look in on yourself, you can only ever detect individual thoughts, memories, experiences. While it is natural to imagine a substantial self that is the subject of these thoughts, he argues this is wrong – the self is no more than the point of view that makes sense of our thoughts and experiences, but cannot itself be given in them.

This idea of the self as a substantial 'thing', which we take to be our essence, causes confusion when we imagine ourselves undergoing brain transplants or being annihilated and reconstituted elsewhere. We assume our personal survival in such thought experiments somehow depends on finding a place for this self. But if we stop thinking in terms of this substantial self, things become clearer. Suppose, for instance, that the teleporter functions correctly in annihilating your body in London but produces two copies on the Moon. Asking which one is you (equivalent to 'where has my self ended up?') is simply asking the wrong question. The outcome is that there are now two human beings, each starting off with exactly the same fund of thoughts, experiences and memories; they will go their own way and their psychological histories will diverge. You (essentially the fund of thoughts, experiences and memories) have survived in the two new individuals – an interesting form of personal survival, achieved at the cost of your personal identity!

the condensed idea
What makes you, you?

11 Other minds

All that Hollywood stuff is utter nonsense. The glazed expression, the fish eyes, the fixed stare – absolute tosh. It's actually really hard to spot a zombie. They look just the same as you and me, walk the same, talk the same – never give a clue that there's nothing going on inside. Give a zombie a good kick on the shin and he'll wince and shriek every bit as loud as you or me. But unlike you and me, he doesn't feel a thing: no pain, no sensation, no consciousness of any kind. Actually, I say 'you and me', but that should really be just 'me'. I am not at all sure about you ... any of you, come to that.

Zombies are frequent guests in the long-running philosophical debate known as the 'problem of other minds'. I know that I have a mind, an inner life of conscious experience, but the content of your mind is completely private and hidden from me; all I can observe directly is your behaviour. Is that sufficient evidence on which to base my belief that you have a mind like mine? To put it more colourfully, how do I know that you are not a zombie like the ones described above – exactly the same as me in terms of behaviour and physiology and yet not conscious?

It may seem absurd to question whether others have minds, but is there anything *irrational* in doing so? Indeed, given the extraordinary difficulty in explaining or accommodating consciousness in a physical world (see page 32), is it not perhaps perfectly reasonable to suppose that the only mind I know – my own – is a great rarity, or even unique? Maybe the rest of you – the zombies – are normal and I am the freak?

Given that we are so similar in other ways...

The most common ways of tackling the problem of other minds, developed by Bertrand Russell amongst others, have been variants of the so-called argument from analogy. I know in my own case that treading on a drawing pin is typically followed by certain kinds of behaviour (saying 'ouch', wincing, and so on) and accompanied by a particular sensation – pain. So I can infer, when other people behave in similar ways in response to similar stimuli, that they too feel pain. More generally, I observe innumerable similarities, both physiological and behavioural, between myself and other people, and I conclude from these similarities that other people are also similar in respect of their psychology.

There is an appealing aura of common sense about the argument from analogy. In the unlikely event of our being called upon to defend our belief in the minds of others, we would probably produce some form of justification along these lines. The argument is inductive, of course (see page 108), so cannot (and is not intended to) provide conclusive proof, but that is also true of much else that we feel justified in believing.

From zombies to mutants

Zombies are not the only guests at conferences on the philosophy of mind. You will also meet mutants. Like zombies, philosophical mutants are less scary than their Hollywood counterparts. Indeed, they are completely indistinguishable from ordinary people when it comes to behaviour and physical makeup. And they even have minds! The catch with mutants is that their minds aren't wired up in quite the same way as yours or mine (well, mine anyway).

There is no limit on how different mutants can be: they may get pleasure from something that would cause me pain, they may see red where I see blue; the only rule is that a mutant's sensations and other mental events are *different* from mine. Mutants are particularly useful when it comes to looking at a different aspect of the other minds problem: not the question of whether other people have minds but whether their minds work in the same way as mine. Can I ever tell, even in principle, that you feel pain as I do? Or how intense your feeling of pain is? Or that your perception of red is the same as mine? With such questions a whole new area of debate opens up; and as with other aspects of the other minds problem, our answers help to elucidate our basic conceptions of what the mind is.

On the face of it, the problem of other minds seems like a case (not unique, in popular estimation) of philosophers finding a problem where the rest of us never even thought of looking. It is true that all of us (even philosophers, for practical reasons at least) take it for granted that others do enjoy an inner life of thoughts and feelings very much like our own. But to reject the philosophical problem on that basis is to miss the point. Nobody is trying to persuade anybody that people are in fact zombies. It is rather that ways we may have of thinking about minds and their relation to bodies leave wide open the *possibility* of zombies. And that should cause us to look seriously at our conceptions of the mind.

Cartesian dualism (see page 28) drives a huge metaphysical wedge between mental and physical events, and it is in the resulting chasm that scepticism about other minds takes root. That is a good reason for looking critically at dualism, whether in Descartes or in its many religious manifestations. Conversely, one of the attractions of physicalist accounts of mind is that mental events can be fully explained, in principle at least, in terms of physical ones; and if the mental dissolves into the physical, zombies vanish at the same time. That doesn't necessarily make such accounts right but it is evidence that they are going in the right direction. In this way, focusing on the problem of other minds can throw light on more general issues within the philosophy of mind.

The usual criticism of the argument is that it involves inference or extrapolation from a single instance (my own mind). Imagine, for instance, that you found an oyster with a pearl inside and inferred from this that all oysters have pearls. To reduce the risk of this kind of mistake, you need to inspect a number of oysters, but this is precisely the course of action that is shut off in the case of other minds. As Ludwig Wittgenstein remarked, 'How can I generalize the one case so irresponsibly?'

The irresponsibility of drawing conclusions on the basis of a single instance is mitigated if the inference is made in a context of relevant background information. For instance, if we recognize that a pearl serves no useful purpose in the functioning of an oyster or that the commercial value of pearls is inconsistent with their ready availability in every oyster, we will be less inclined to draw false inferences from our single specimen.

The problem with minds and consciousness is that they remain so mysterious, so unlike anything else that we are familiar with, that it is altogether unclear what might count as relevant background information. To this extent the problem of other minds can be seen as another symptom of the more general mind–body problem. If our theory of mind can demystify the relation between mental and physical phenomena, it may be hoped that our concerns over other minds will diminish or vanish altogether (see box opposite).

the condensed idea
Is there anybody there?

12 Hume's guillotine

‘ In every system of morality, which I have hitherto met with, I have remarked, that the author proceeds for some time in the ordinary way of reasoning, and establishes the being of a God, or makes observations concerning human affairs; when of a sudden I am surprized to find, that instead of the usual copulations of propositions, is, and is not, I meet with no proposition that is not connected with an ought, or an ought not…

…This change is imperceptible; but is, however, of the last consequence. For as this *ought*, or *ought not*, expresses some new relation or affirmation, 'tis necessary that it should be observed and explained; and at the same time that a reason should be given, for what seemed altogether inconceivable, how this new relation can be a deduction from others, which are entirely different from it.’

In this celebrated passage from his *Treatise of Human Nature*, the Scottish philosopher David Hume gives, in his usual laconic manner, the classic formulation of what has since remained one of the central questions in moral philosophy. How can we possibly move from a *descriptive* statement about how things stand in the world (an 'is' statement) to a *prescriptive* statement telling us what ought to be done (an 'ought' statement)? Or put briefly, how can we derive an 'ought' from an 'is'? Hume evidently thinks that we cannot and many thinkers have agreed with him, believing that 'Hume's guillotine' (or more prosaically, 'Hume's law') has decisively severed the world of fact from the world of value.

The naturalistic fallacy

Hume's law is often confused with a related but distinct view put forward by the English philosopher G.E. Moore in his *Principia Ethica* (1903). Moore accused earlier philosophers of committing what he called the 'naturalistic fallacy', which involves *identifying* ethical concepts with natural concepts; thus 'good', for instance, is taken to *mean the same thing as* (say) 'pleasurable'. But, Moore alleged, it is still an open question to ask whether what is pleasurable is also good – the question is not vacuous – so the identification must be mistaken.

Moore's own view (which has been much less influential than the supposed fallacy that he identified) was that ethical terms such as 'good' are 'non-natural' properties – simple and unanalysable properties, accessible only by means of a special moral sense known as 'intuition'. To confuse matters further, the expression 'naturalistic fallacy' is sometimes used for the completely different mistake – much beloved of advertisers – of claiming that the fact that something is natural (or unnatural) provides sufficient grounds for supposing that it is also good (or bad). Victims of natural pathogens undergoing treatment with synthetic drugs would readily testify to the flawed nature of this argument.

Value in a value-free world

The problem that Hume has highlighted is due in part to two strong but conflicting convictions that many of us share. On the one hand, we believe that we live in a physical world that can in principle be fully explained by laws discoverable by science; a world of objective fact from which value is excluded. On the other hand, we feel that in making moral judgements, for instance that genocide is wrong, we are stating something true about the world; something that we can know and which would be true anyway, irrespective of how we might feel about it. But these views appear to be incompatible if we accept Hume's law; and if we cannot ground our moral evaluations in the value-free world described by science, we are apparently forced back upon our own feelings and preferences and must look within ourselves to find the origins of our moral sentiments. Hume himself was not unaware of the significance of his observation, believing that if proper heed were given to it 'all the vulgar systems of morality' would be subverted. The logically unbridgeable gap between fact and value that Hume seems to open up casts doubt over the very status of ethical claims and thus lies at the heart of moral philosophy.

Ethics, or moral philosophy, is often divided into three broad areas. At the most general level, **meta-ethics** investigates the source or basis of morality, including such questions as whether it is essentially objective or subjective in nature. **Normative ethics** focuses on the ethical standards (or norms) on which moral conduct is based; thus utilitarianism, for instance, is a normative system based on the standard of 'utility'. Finally, at the lowest level, **applied ethics** brings philosophical theory to bear on practical issues, such as abortion, euthanasia, just war and the treatment of animals. Philosophers have taken an array of positions on all these questions; and with these come many -isms. The following gives a thumbnail sketch of some of the most commonly encountered of these ethical positions.

- **An absolutist** holds that certain actions are right or wrong under any circumstances.

- **A consequentialist** maintains that the rightness or wrongness of actions can be assessed purely by reference to their effectiveness in bringing about certain desirable ends or states of affairs. The best-known consequentialist system is **utilitarianism** (see page 69).

- **A deontologist** considers certain actions to be intrinsically right or wrong, irrespective of their consequences; particular significance is usually attached to an agent's intentions and to the notions of duties and rights. **Kantian ethics** (see page 72) is the most important deontological system.

- **A naturalist** believes that ethical concepts can be explained or analysed purely in terms of 'facts of nature' that are discoverable by science, most often facts about human psychology such as pleasure.

- **A non-cognitivist** holds that morality is not a matter of knowledge, because the business of moralizing does not deal in *facts* at all; instead, a moral judgement expresses the attitudes, emotions, and so on, of the person making it. Examples of non-cognitive positions are **emotivism** and **prescriptivism** (see page 62).

- **An objectivist** holds that moral values and properties are part of the 'furniture (or fabric) of the universe', existing independently of any human that may apprehend them; ethical claims are not subjective or relative to anything else, and may be true or false according to whether they accurately reflect the way things stand in the world. Objectivism holds that ethical concepts are metaphysically real and hence is largely coextensive with moral realism.

- **A subjectivist** holds that value is grounded not in external reality but either in our beliefs about reality or in our emotional reactions to it. The latter position is basically equivalent to that of non-cognitivism (see above). In the former case (a cognitive position), the subjectivist maintains that there are ethical facts but denies that these are objectively true or false; an example of this form of subjectivism is **relativism** (see page 52).

the condensed idea
The is–ought gap

13 One man's meat …

'**W**hen Darius was king of Persia, he summoned the Greeks who happened to be present at his court, and asked them what they would take to eat the dead bodies of their fathers. They replied that they would not do it for any money in the world. Later, in the presence of the Greeks, and through an interpreter, so that they could understand, he asked some Indians, of the tribe called Callatiae, who do in fact eat their parents' dead bodies, what they would take to burn them [as was the Greek custom]. They uttered a cry of horror and forbade him to mention such a dreadful thing.'

So who has got it right, the Greeks or the Callatians? We might blanch a little at the prospect of eating our parents, but no more than the Callatians would blanch at burning theirs. In the end we would surely agree with Herodotus, the Greek historian recounting this story, when he approvingly quotes the poet Pindar – 'Custom is king of all'. It isn't a matter of one side being right and the other wrong; there is no 'right answer'. Each group has its own code of customs and traditions; each is behaving correctly according to its own code, and it is to this code that each would appeal in defending its respective funeral arrangements.

In this case what is morally right doesn't appear to be absolute, one way or the other – it is relative to the culture and traditions of the social groups concerned. And there are of course countless other examples of such cultural diversity, both geographical and historical. It is from cases such as these that the relativist argues that in general there are no absolute or universal truths: all moral appraisals and assessments should only be made relative to the social norms of the groups involved.

Vive la différence

The relativist's proposal is in effect that we treat moral judgements as if they were aesthetic ones. In matters of taste, it is generally not appropriate to talk of error: *de gustibus non disputandum* – 'over tastes let there be no dispute'. If you say you like tomatoes and I don't, we agree to differ: something is right or true for you but not for me. In such cases truth tracks sincerity: if I sincerely say that I like something, I cannot be wrong – it is true (for me). So following this analogy, if we (as a society) approve of capital punishment, it is morally right (for us), and it is not something that we can be wrong about. And just as we would not try to persuade people to stop liking tomatoes or criticize them for doing so, in the moral case persuasion or criticism would be inappropriate. In fact, of course, our moral life is full of argument and censure, and we habitually take strong positions on matters such as capital punishment. We may even take issue with *ourselves* over time: I can change my mind over a moral question, and we may collectively shift our stance, for example in a matter such as slavery. The out-and-out relativist would have to say that one thing was right for some people but not others, or right for me (or us) at one time but not at another. And in the case of slavery, female circumcision, legal infanticide, and so on, this might be a bitter pill for the relativist to swallow.

This failure of relativism to take any serious account of aspects that are so clearly characteristic of our actual moral lives is usually seen as a decisive blow against the thesis, but relativists may try to turn it to their advantage. Perhaps, they would argue, we should not be so judgemental and critical of others. Indeed, the lesson from the Greeks and the Callatians is that we need to be more tolerant of others, more open-minded, more sensitive to other customs and practices. This line of argument has led many to associate relativism with tolerance and open-mindedness, and by contrast non relativists are portrayed as being intolerant and impatient of practices other than their own. Taken to an extreme, it leads to a picture of the Western cultural imperialist arrogantly imposing his views on benighted others. But this is a caricature: there is in fact no incompatibility between taking a generally tolerant view of things and yet maintaining that on some matters other people or other cultures have got it wrong. Indeed, a frustration facing the relativist is that it is only the non-relativist who can hold up tolerance and cultural sensitivity as universal virtues (see box on page 54)!

Getting knowledge in perspective

The absurdity of full-blown relativism and the perils of its wide-spread adoption as a political mantra (see boxes on page 54 and 55) have meant that insights offered by a more temperate form of relativism are sometimes overlooked. The most important lesson of relativism is that

Running rings round relativism

Strong or radical relativism – the idea that all claims (moral and everything else) are relative – quickly ties itself in knots. Is the claim that all claims are relative itself relative? Well, it has to be, to avoid self-contradiction; but if it is, it means that my claims that all claims are absolute is true *for me*. And this kind of incoherence rapidly infects everything else. Relativists can't say it is always wrong to criticize the cultural arrangements of other societies, as it may be right *for me* to do so. And they can't maintain that it is always right to be tolerant and open-minded, as it may be right for some autocrat to stamp out all signs of dissent. In general, relativists cannot, consistently and without hypocrisy, maintain the validity of their own position. The self-refuting nature of full-blown relativism was spotted in its infancy by Plato, who swiftly showed up the inconsistencies in the relativist position adopted by the sophist Protagoras (in the dialogue that bears his name). The lesson of all this is that rational discussion depends on sharing *some* common ground; we have to agree on *something*, to have some common truth, in order to communicate meaningfully. But it is precisely this common ground that is denied by radical relativism.

knowledge itself is perspectival: our take on the world is always from a certain perspective or point of view; there is no external vantage point from which we can observe the world 'as it really is' or 'as it is anyway'. This point is often explained in terms of conceptual schemes or frameworks: put simply, we can only get an intellectual grasp on reality from within our own conceptual framework, determined by a complex combination of factors including our culture and history. But the fact that we cannot step back from, or outside of, our particular conceptual scheme and take an objective view of things – a 'god's-eye view' – does not mean that we cannot get to know anything. A perspective has to be a perspective on *something*, and by sharing and comparing our different perspectives we can hope to bring our various beliefs into relief and to achieve a fuller, rounder, more 'stereoscopic' picture of the world. This benign image suggests that progress towards understanding is to be made through collaboration, communication and interchange of ideas and opinions: a positive legacy of relativism.

the condensed idea
Is it all relative?

14 The divine command theory

Questions of right and wrong, good and bad, virtue and vice are the kinds of things that we might expect to lose sleep over: abortion, euthanasia, human rights, treatment of animals, stem cell research … a never-ending list of perilous and supercharged issues. More than any other area, ethics feels like a minefield – treacherous terrain where you expect to be tripped up at any moment, yet where stumbling might prove very costly.

Paradoxically, though, for many people the business of moralizing is, on the face of it, more like a stroll in the park. In the minds of millions of people morality is inextricably tied up with religion: this or that is right or wrong for the simple reason that God (or a god) has ordained that it should be so; good is good and bad is bad because God says so.

> **'Is the pious loved by the gods because it is pious, or is it pious because they love it?'**
> Plato, c.375 Bc

In each of the three 'religions of the Book' – Judaism, Christianity and Islam – the system of morality is based on 'divine command': it is for God to command, humans to obey; God imposes on its worshippers a set of moral injunctions; virtuous behaviour requires obedience, while disobedience is sin. Surely such a code of ethical rules, underwritten by God's own hand, should banish the concerns that beset subjectivist accounts of morality – the nasty suspicion that we are making up the rules as we go along?

The Euthyphro dilemma

Without God, of course, the divine command theory immediately collapses (see box on page 58), but even allowing that God does exist, there are still a number of serious problems threatening the theory. Probably the gravest of these is the so-called Euthyphro dilemma, first raised by Plato some 2,400 years ago in his dialogue *Euthyphro*. Socrates (Plato's mouthpiece in his dialogues) engages a young man named Euthyphro in a discussion of the nature of piety. They agree

Making sense of God's commands

The Euthyphro dilemma aside, another serious difficulty facing those who would base morality on divine command is that the various religious texts that are the principal means by which God's will is made known to humans contain many conflicting and/or unpalatable messages. To take a notorious example from the Bible, the book of Leviticus (20:13) states that: 'If a man lies with a male as with a woman, both of them have committed an abomination; they shall surely be put to death; their blood is upon them.' If the Bible is the word of God and the word of God determines what is moral, the execution of sexually active homosexual males is morally sanctioned. But most people today would regard such a view as morally abhorrent, and it is in any case inconsistent with injunctions elsewhere in the Bible (most obviously, the commandment not to kill). Clearly, it is a challenge for the divine command theorist to use God's known views to construct a generally acceptable and internally coherent moral system.

that piety is 'whatever is loved by the gods', but then Socrates poses a crucial question: are pious things pious because they are loved by the gods, or are they loved by the gods because they are pious? It is on the horns of this dilemma (usually expressed in monotheistic terms) that the divine command theory is caught.

So, is what is good good because God commands it, or does God command it because it is good? Neither alternative is very palatable to the divine command theorist. Taking the first part first: killing (say) happens to be wrong because God commands it, but things might have been otherwise. God might have ordained that killing is OK or even obligatory, and it would have been – just because God said so. On this reading religious observance adds up to little more than blind obedience to an arbitrary authority. So does the other alternative fare any better? Not really. If God commands what is good because it is good, clearly its goodness is independent of God. At best God's role is that of moral messenger, passing on ethical prescriptions but not the source of them. So we could go straight to the source and happily shoot the messenger. At least in the role of moral lawmaker, God is redundant. So when it comes to morality, either God is arbitrary or God is irrelevant. Not an easy choice for those seeking to make God the guarantor or sanction of their ethics.

> 'No morality can be founded on authority, Even if the authority were divine'
>
> A.J.Ayer, 1968

A common counterattack on the Euthyphro dilemma is to insist that 'God is good' and therefore that it would not command evil. But this line of attack risks circularity or incoherence. If 'good' means 'commanded by God', 'God is good' will be virtually meaningless – something like 'God is such that it complies with its own commands'.

Lost in action?

The biggest danger facing the divine command theory is the risk of losing its divine commander: we may be less than fully persuaded by the various arguments put forward to prove the existence of God and we may not have the benefit of faith (see page 172). Undaunted, some advocates of the theory have ingeniously turned the danger to their advantage, using it as a *proof* of God's existence:

1. There is such a thing as morality – we have a code of ethical laws/commands.
2. God is the only candidate for the role of lawmaker/ commander. So ...
3. God must exist.

This line of reasoning is unlikely to win over an opponent, however. The first premise, implying that morality is essentially something that exists independently of humans, begs one of the most basic underlying questions. And even allowing that morality does exist independently of us, the second premise has to bear the full brunt of the Euthyphro attack.

More promising, perhaps, is to take the phrase to mean 'God is (identical with) good(ness)' and therefore that its commands will inevitably be good. But if Godness and goodness are one and the same, 'God is good' is utterly vacuous: no light has been shed and we have gone in a circle – an example, perhaps, of God's fondness for moving in mysterious ways.

the condensed idea
Because God says so

15 The boo/hoorah theory

'**A**nd Moses was there with the Lord forty days and forty nights; he did neither eat bread, nor drink water. And he wrote upon the tablets the words of the covenant, the ten commandments: 'Hoorah! to having no other gods before me.

'Boo! to making unto thee any graven image.

[*five boos and two hoorahs follow; then …*]

'Boo! to coveting thy neighbour's wife, or his manservant, or his maidservant, or his ox, or his ass, or any thing that is thy neighbour's.'

So spake the Lord, according to emotivism, or the 'boo/hoorah theory' of ethics. Put like this, emotivism may not seem like a very serious attempt to represent the force of ethical assertions – and the feeling is doubtless reinforced by the tongue-in-cheek nickname. In fact, however, emotivism is a highly influential theory with a distinguished history, and it is motivated by deep concerns over what may seem a more commonsensical understanding of our moral lives.

The shift to subjectivism

There are different kinds of facts in the world that are objectively true – facts whose truth does not depend on us. Some of these are scientific, describing physical events, processes and relations; others are moral, describing things in the world that are right and wrong, good and bad. Such a picture may appeal to common sense, perhaps, but it has proved far less attractive to many philosophers.

Take a putatively moral fact: killing is wrong. We can describe an act of killing in minute detail, citing all sorts of physical and psychological facts to explain how and why it was done. But what further property or quality are we adding to the picture when we ascribe wrongness to it? Basically we are saying that killing is the kind of thing we *shouldn't* do – that amongst all the other things we may truly say of killing, it also has an intrinsic property of 'not-to-be-doneness'. Struck by the sheer oddity of finding such a property in the world (the supposedly value-free world described by science; see page 132), many philosophers propose that we replace the notion of objective moral properties existing in the world with some kind of subjective response to things in the world.

Reason, slave of the passions

The chief inspiration for modern forms of moral subjectivism is the Scottish philosopher David Hume. His famous plea for a subjectivist account of morality appears in his *Treatise of Human Nature*:

'Take any action allowed to be vicious: Wilful murder, for instance. Examine it in all lights, and see if you can find that matter of fact, or real existence, which you call vice. In whichever way you take it, you find only certain passions, motives, volitions and thoughts. There is no other matter of fact in the case. The vice entirely escapes you, as long as you consider the object. You never can find it, until you turn your reflection into your own breast, and find a sentiment of disapprobation, which arises in you, towards this action. Here is a matter of fact; but 'tis the object of feeling, not of reason. It lies in yourself, not in the object.'

According to Hume's own account of moral action, all humans are naturally moved by a 'moral sense' or 'sympathy', which is essentially a capacity to share the feelings of happiness or misery of others; and it is this sentiment, rather than reason, that provides the motive for our moral actions. Reason is essential in understanding the consequences of our actions and in rationally planning how to achieve our moral aims, but it is itself inert and unable to provide any impetus to action: in Hume's famous phrase, 'reason is, and ought only to be the slave of the passions'.

From description to expression

According to a naïve subjectivist view, moral assertions are simply descriptions or reports of our feelings about the way things are in the world. So when I say 'Murder is wrong', I am simply stating my (or perhaps my community's) disapproval of it. But this is too simple. If I say 'Murder is right' and that is an accurate description of my feelings, then that will be true too. Moral disagreement is apparently impossible. Something more sophisticated is needed.

Emotivism (or expressivism) – the boo/hoorah theory – is a more subtle form of subjectivism, suggesting that moral judgements are not descriptions or statements of our feelings about the world but expressions of those feelings. So, when we make a moral judgement,

Prescriptivism

The most common criticism of emotivism is that it fails to capture the logic of ethical discourse – the characteristic patterns of reasoning and rational argument that underlie it. Success in this respect is considered to be one of the chief recommendations of a rival subjectivist theory known as prescriptivism, closely associated with the English philosopher R.M. Hare. Taking as its starting point the insight that moral terms have a prescriptive element – they tell us what to do or how to behave – prescriptivism proposes that the essence of moral terms is that they are action-guiding; saying that killing is wrong is equivalent to giving and accepting a command – 'Don't kill!' According to Hare's account, the feature of ethical judgements that distinguishes them from other kinds of command is that they are 'universalizable': if I issue a moral injunction, I am thereby committed to holding that that injunction should be obeyed by anyone (including myself) in relevantly similar circumstances (that is, I must comply with the golden rule; see page 76). Moral disagreement, the prescriptivist proposes, is analogous to giving conflicting commands; inconsistency and indecision are explained by there being several injunctions, not all of which can be simultaneously obeyed. In this way prescriptivism apparently allows more space for disagreement and debate than emotivism does, though some still question whether it really mirrors the full complexity of moral dialogue.

we are expressing an emotional response – our approbation ('hoorah!') or disapprobation ('boo!') of something in the world. 'Killing is wrong' is an expression of our disapproval ('boo to murder!'); 'it is good to tell the truth' is an expression of our approval ('hoorah for truth-telling!').

The big problem for emotivists is to bring their theory into some sort of alignment with the way that we actually think about and conduct our moral discourse. This discourse presupposes an external world of objective values: we deliberate and argue about moral questions; we appeal to moral (and other) facts in order to settle them;

we make ethical claims that may be true or false; and there are moral truths that we may come to know. But according to the emotivist, there is nothing ethical to know – we are not making claims at all but expressing our feelings, and such expressions cannot of course be true or false. The emotivist may allow that deliberation and disagreement are possible over our background beliefs and the context of our actions, but it is difficult to flesh this out into something like our normal conception of moral debate. The logical connections between moral assertions themselves appear to be missing, and moral reasoning is apparently little more than an exercise in rhetoric – morality as advertising, as it has been caustically put.

The staunch response to this is simply to bite the bullet: yes, the emotivist may say, the theory does not square with our usual assumptions, but that is because the assumptions are wrong, not the theory. According to this so-called 'error theory', our normal ethical discourse is simply mistaken, because it is based on objective moral facts that do not actually exist. Many attempts have been made to bring the emotivist picture closer to our realist-sounding ethical discourse, but for many the gap is still too wide and other approaches have been proposed. Probably the most important of these alternatives is prescriptivism (see box opposite).

the condensed idea
Expressing moral judgements

16 Ends and means

'**M**r Quelch wasn't altogether certain whether sharks had lips and, if they did, whether they could lick them; but he had no doubt at all that if they did and could, that is exactly what they were now doing. The balloon was now falling faster towards the sea, and he could clearly see the many fins of the assembled diners cutting menacingly through the water …

… Mr Quelch knew that in the next two minutes he himself and the cream of Greyfriars would be shark bait – unless they could jettison more ballast. But everything had already been thrown out of the basket – all that was left was himself and the six boys. It was perfectly clear that only Bunter was of sufficient bulk to save the day. Hard cheese for the Fat Owl of the Remove, but there really was no other way …

' "Oh, crikey … oh really, you fellows … look here, if you lay a finger on me I'll … Yarooooh!" '

Let's suppose that Quelch's assessment of the situation is entirely accurate. There really are only two options: all six boys (including Bunter) and Quelch himself fall into the sea and are torn to shreds by sharks; or Bunter alone is thrown into the sea and eaten. Apart from the unpleasantness of being tossed out of the balloon, it makes little difference to Bunter, who will die either way, but by throwing Bunter out, Quelch can save himself and the five other boys. So is he right to sacrifice Bunter? Does the end (saving several innocent lives) justify the means (taking one innocent life)?

An ethical divide

Such decisions involving life and death are not, of course, merely the stuff of fiction. In real life, people sometimes find themselves in situations where it is necessary to allow one or a few innocent individuals to die, or in extreme cases even to kill them, in order to save several or many innocent lives. These are cases that test our intuitions to the limit, wrenching us sharply one way or the other – and sometimes in both directions at the same time.

This fundamental uncertainty is mirrored in the very different approaches that philosophers have taken in trying to explain such dilemmas. The various theories that have been proposed are often seen as sitting on one or other side of a major fault line in ethics – the line that separates duty-based (deontological) theories from consequence-based (consequentialist) ones.

Consequentialism and deontology

One way of highlighting the differences between consequentialism and deontology is in terms of ends and means. A consequentialist proposes that the question of whether an action is right or wrong should be determined purely on the basis of its consequences; an action is regarded merely as a means to some desirable end, and its rightness or wrongness is a measure of how effective it is in achieving that end. The end itself is some state of affairs (such as a state of happiness) that results from, or is consequent upon, the various actions that contribute to it. In choosing between various available courses of action, consequentialists will merely weigh up the good and bad consequences in each case and make their decisions on that basis. In the Bunter case, for instance, they are likely to judge that the good outcome in terms of innocent lives saved is justification for the taking of one life.

By contrast, in a deontological system actions are not seen merely as means to an end but as right or wrong in themselves. Actions are thought to have intrinsic value in their own right, not just instrumental value in contributing towards some desirable end. For instance, the deontologist may rule that killing innocent people is intrinsically wrong: the jettisoning of Bunter is wrong in itself and cannot be justified by any good consequences it is supposed to have.

The Billy Bunter case may seem far-fetched, but nasty dilemmas of this kind do sometimes arise in real life. All the cases in this chapter are similar, at least in the ethical questions they raise, to events that actually occurred and are certain to occur again. The best-known consequentialist theory is utilitarianism (see page 69); the most influential deontological system is that developed by Kant (see page 72).

An airliner carrying 120 passengers is hurtling out of control towards a densely populated area. There is no time to evacuate the area and the impact of the plane is certain to kill thousands. The only possible move is to shoot down the plane. Should you do it?

Conjoined (Siamese) twins are both certain to die within months unless they are surgically separated. The necessary operation offers excellent prospects of one twin living a reasonably healthy and fulfilled life but will result in the death of the other twin. Do you proceed? (Do you do so even if the parents do not give their consent?)

Patient A is terminally ill and certain to die within a week. His heart and kidneys are a perfect match for patients B and C, who are certain to die before him if they do not get the transplants they need but who have good prospects of recovery if they do. No other donors are available. Do you kill patient A (with his permission, without his permission?) in order to save patients B and C?

A Gestapo officer rounds up 10 children and threatens to shoot them unless you reveal the identity and whereabouts of a spy. As it happens, you didn't know that there was a spy, let alone his or her identity, but you are quite certain both that the officer won't believe you if you plead ignorance and that he will carry out his threat. Do you name someone – anyone – to save the children? (How do you decide who?)

You, together with the other passengers and crew of a small aeroplane, survive a crash on a desolate mountainside. There is no food, no chance of escaping on foot, and no prospect of a rescue party reaching you for several weeks, by which time you will all have starved to death. The meat from one passenger will sustain the others until help arrives. Do you kill and eat one of your companions? (How do you choose?)

The end justifies the means

In a trivial sense, a means can only ever be justified by an end, as the former is by definition a way of achieving the latter; so a means is justified (that is, validated as a means) by the very fact of achieving its intended end. Problems can arise – and the maxim could be seen as sinister – when an inappropriate end is chosen and the choice is made in the light of ideology or dogma. If a political ideologue, for instance, or a religious zealot sets up a particular end as important to the exclusion of all others, it is a short step for their followers to conclude that it is morally acceptable to use any means whatsoever to achieve that end.

the condensed idea
The least bad option

17 The experience machine

'Suppose there were an experience machine that would give you any experience you desired. Superduper neuropsychologists could stimulate your brain so that you would think and feel you were writing a great novel, or making a friend, or reading an interesting book. All the time you would be floating in a tank, with electrodes attached to your brain. Should you plug into this machine for life, preprogramming your life's desires? ... Of course, while in the tank you won't know that you're there; you'll think it's all actually happening ... Would you plug in? What else can matter to us, other than how our lives feel from the inside?'

The creator of this thought experiment from 1974, the US philosopher Robert Nozick, thinks that the answers to his closing questions are, respectively, 'No' and 'A lot'. Superficially, the experience machine looks a lot like Putnam's vat for the brain (see page 4). Both describe virtual realities in which a world is simulated in such a way that it is completely indistinguishable, from the inside at least, from real life. But while Putnam's interest is in the situation of the brain within the vat and what that tells us about the limits of scepticism, Nozick's main concern is with the situation of a person before they are attached to his machine: would they choose a life plugged into the machine and, if they did, what can we learn from their choice?

The choice is between a simulated life of unalloyed pleasure in which every ambition and desire is achieved; and a real life marked by all the expected frustrations and disappointments, the usual mixture of partial successes and unfulfilled dreams. In spite of the obvious attractions of life attached to the experience machine, most people, Nozick thinks, would choose *not* to be plugged into it. The *reality* of life is important: we want to do certain things, not only experience the pleasure of doing them. Yet, if pleasure were the only thing affecting our well-being, if it were the sole constituent of the good life, surely we would not make this choice, since far more pleasure would be had by being plugged into the experience machine. From this, Nozick infers that there are other things apart from pleasure that we consider intrinsically valuable.

Classical utilitarianism

This conclusion is damaging to any hedonistic (pleasure-based) theory of ethics, and in particular to utilitarianism, at least in the classic formulation given by its founder Jeremy Bentham in the 18th century. Utilitarianism is the view that actions should be judged right or wrong to the extent that they increase or decrease human well-being or 'utility'. Several interpretations of utility have been proposed since Bentham's time, but for him it consisted in human pleasure or happiness, and his theory of right action is sometimes summarized as the promotion of 'the greatest happiness of the greatest number'.

Utilitarianism doesn't shy away from moral conclusions that run counter to our normal intuitions (see page 64). Indeed, one of its chief recommendations for Bentham was that it would provide a rational and scientific basis for moral and social decision-making, in contrast to the chaotic and incoherent intuitions on which so-called natural rights and natural law were based. In order to establish such a rational basis, Bentham proposed a 'felicific calculus', according to which the different amounts of pleasure and pain produced by different actions could be measured and compared; the right action on a given occasion could then be determined by a simple process of addition and subtraction. Thus for Bentham different pleasures differ only in respect of duration and intensity, not in quality; a rather monolithic conception of pleasure that looks vulnerable to the implications of Nozick's experience machine. Given his uncompromising nature, we may guess that Bentham would have happily trampled on the intuition that Nozick's thought experiment draws out. J.S. Mill, however, another of utilitarianism's founding fathers, was more concerned to knock off some of the theory's rougher edges.

Higher and lower pleasures

Contemporary critics were quick to point out just how narrow a conception of morality Bentham had given. By supposing that life had no higher end than pleasure, he had apparently left out of the reckoning all sorts of things that we would normally count as inherently valuable, such as knowledge, honour and achievement; he had proposed (as Mill reports the charge) 'a doctrine worthy only of swine'. Bentham himself, in splendidly egalitarian fashion, confronted the accusation head-on: 'Prejudice apart,' he declared, 'the game of

Varieties of utilitarianism

Utilitarianism is, historically, the most significant version of consequentialism, the view that actions should be judged right or wrong in the light of their consequences (see page 65). In the case of utilitarianism, the value of actions is determined by their contribution to well-being or 'utility'. In the classical (hedonic) utilitarianism of Bentham and Mill, utility is understood as human pleasure, but this has since been modified and broadened in various ways. These different approaches typically recognize that human happiness depends not only on pleasure but also on the satisfaction of a wide range of desires and preferences. Some theorists have also proposed extending the scope of utilitarianism beyond human well-being to other forms of sentient life.

There are also different views on how utilitarianism is to be applied to actions. According to **direct** or **act utilitarianism**, each action is assessed directly in terms of its own contribution to utility. In contrast, according to **rule utilitarianism**, an appropriate course of action is determined by reference to various sets of rules which will, if generally followed, promote utility. For instance, killing an innocent person might in certain circumstances lead to the saving of many lives and hence increase general utility, so for the act utilitarian this would be the right course of action. However, *as a rule* killing innocent people decreases utility, so the rule utilitarian might hold that the same action was wrong, even though it might have beneficial consequences on a particular occasion. Rule utilitarianism may thus accord more closely with our common intuitions on moral matters, though this has not necessarily commended it to most recent utilitarian thinkers, who for various reasons regard it as incoherent or otherwise objectionable.

push-pin is of equal value with the arts and sciences of music and poetry'. In other words, if a greater overall quantity of pleasure was produced by playing a popular game, that game was indeed more valuable than the more refined pursuits of the intellect.

Mill was uncomfortable with Bentham's forthright conclusion and sought to modify utilitarianism to deflect the critics' charge. In addition to Bentham's two variables in measuring pleasure – duration and intensity – Mill allowed a third – quality – thereby introducing a hierarchy of higher and lower pleasures. According to this distinction, some pleasures, such as those of the intellect and the arts, are by their nature more valuable than base physical ones, and by giving them greater weight in the calculus of pleasure, Mill was able to conclude that 'the life of Socrates dissatisfied is better than that of a fool satisfied'. This accommodation is made at some cost, however. At the very least, one of the apparent attractions of Bentham's scheme – its simplicity – is diminished, although the operation of the felicific calculus is in fact fraught with difficulty in any case. More seriously, Mill's notion of different kinds of pleasure seems to require some criterion other than pleasure to tell them apart. If something other than pleasure is a constituent of Mill's idea of utility, it may help him in resisting the kind of problem raised by Nozick, but it then becomes questionable whether his theory remains strictly utilitarian at all.

the condensed idea
Is happiness enough?

18 The categorical imperative

You know that Christina wants to kill your friend Mariah, who you have just left sitting at the bar. Christina comes up to you and asks if you know where Mariah is. If you tell her the truth, Christina will find Mariah and kill her. If you lie and tell her that you saw Mariah leaving five minutes ago, Christina will be thrown off the scent, allowing Mariah to get away. What should you do? Tell the truth or tell a lie?

It seems crazy even to ask the question. The consequences of telling the truth are dreadful. Of course you should lie – a very white lie, you may think, in a very good cause. But in the view of Immanuel Kant – one of the most influential and, some would say, the greatest philosopher of the past 300 years – that is not the right answer. Not lying is, according to Kant, a fundamental principle of morality, or 'categorical imperative': something that one is obliged to do, unconditionally and regardless of the consequences. This implacable insistence on duty, together with the notion of the categorical imperative that underlies it, is the cornerstone of Kantian ethics.

Hypothetical versus categorical imperatives

To explain what a categorical imperative is, Kant first tells us what it isn't, by contrasting it with a *hypothetical* imperative. Suppose I tell you what to do by issuing an order (an imperative): 'Stop smoking!' Implicitly, there is a string of conditions that I might attach to this command – 'if you don't want to ruin your health', for instance, or 'if you don't want to waste your money'. Of course, if you are unconcerned about your health and money, the order carries no weight and you need not comply. With a categorical imperative, by contrast, there are no ifs attached, implicit or explicit. 'Don't lie!' and 'Don't kill people!' are injunctions that are not hypothesized on any aim or desire that you may or may not have and must be obeyed as a matter of duty, absolutely and unconditionally. A categorical imperative of this kind, unlike a hypothetical imperative, constitutes a moral law.

In Kant's view, beneath every action there is an underlying rule of conduct, or maxim. Such maxims can have the form of categorical imperatives, however, without qualifying as moral laws, because they fail to pass a test, which is itself a supreme or overarching form of categorical imperative:

> *Act only in accordance with a maxim that you can at the same time will to become a universal law.*

In other words, an action is morally permissible only if it accords with a rule that you can consistently and universally apply to yourself and others (in effect, a variant of the golden rule; see page 76). For instance, we might propose a maxim that it is permissible to lie. But lying is only possible against a background of (some level of) truth-telling – if everyone lied all the time, no one would believe anyone – and for that reason it would be self-defeating and in some sense irrational to wish for lying to become a universal law. Likewise, stealing presupposes a context of property ownership, but the whole concept of property would collapse if *everybody* stole; breaking promises presupposes a generally accepted institution of promise-keeping; and so on.

The requirement of universality thus rules out certain kinds of conduct on logical grounds, but there seem to be many others that we could universalize, yet would not wish to count as moral. 'Always look after your own interests', 'Break promises where you can do so without undermining the institution of promising' – there doesn't appear to be anything inconsistent or irrational in willing that these should become universal laws. So how does Kant head off this danger?

Autonomy and pure reason

The demands of the categorical imperative impose a rational structure on Kant's ethics, but the task is then to move from logical framework to actual moral content – to explain how 'pure reason', without empirical support, can inform and direct the will of a moral agent. The answer lies in the inherent value of moral agency itself – value based on the 'single supreme principle of morality', the freedom or autonomy of a will that obeys laws that it imposes on itself. The supreme importance attached to autonomous, free-willed agents is mirrored in the second great formulation of the categorical imperative:

Act in such a way that you always treat humanity,
whether in your own person or in the person of any other, never simply
as a means, but always at the same time as an end.

Once the inestimable value of one's own moral agency is recognized, it is necessary to extend that respect to the agency of others. To treat others merely as a means to promote one's own interests undermines or destroys their agency, so maxims that are self-serving or damaging to others contravene this formulation of the categorical imperative and do not qualify as moral laws. In essence, there is a recognition here that there are basic rights that belong to people by virtue of their humanity and that may not be overridden: a profoundly humane and enlightened facet of Kantian ethics.

the condensed idea
Duty at any cost

19 The golden rule

'**T**he heart of the question is whether all Americans are to be afforded equal rights and equal opportunities, whether we are going to treat our fellow Americans as we want to be treated. If an American, because his skin is dark, cannot eat lunch in a restaurant open to the public, if he cannot send his children to the best public school available, if he cannot vote for the public officials who will represent him, if, in short, he cannot enjoy the full and free life which all of us want, then who among us would be content to have the color of his skin changed and stand in his place? Who among us would then be content with the counsels of patience and delay?'

In June 1963, at a time when racial tension and hatred in the USA were spilling over into overt violence and public demonstration, President John F. Kennedy made a speech to the American people arguing passionately against segregation and discrimination on grounds of race. At the heart of his speech was an appeal to one of the most fundamental and ubiquitous of all moral principles, the so-called 'golden rule'. Encapsulated in the saying 'Do unto others as you would have them do unto you', the underlying notion seems to be central to the most basic human ethical sense and is expressed in some variant or other in virtually every religious and moral tradition.

Few moral philosophers have failed to invoke the golden rule or at least to remark on its relation to principles of their own theories. Although Kant claimed that the golden rule lacked the rigour to qualify as a universal law, there are clearly echoes of it in the most famous formulation of his categorical imperative: 'Act only in accordance with a maxim that you can at the same time will to become a universal law' (see page 74). At the other end of the philosophical spectrum, J.S. Mill claimed the golden rule for utilitarianism (see page 69). A more recent example is to be found in prescriptivism, the ethical theory developed by R.M. Hare, who proposes that the notion of 'universalizability' is an essential property of moral judgements.

Making sense of the golden rule

In spite of its intuitive appeal, it is less clear how much practical guidance can actually be gleaned from the golden rule. Its sheer

Free-riders and hypocrites

Not-so-distant cousins of golden-rule flouters – those who wish to do but are less happy to be done by – are free-riders, whose aim is to enjoy the benefit of being done by without incurring the cost of doing. Workers who do not join a union but benefit from a pay rise won by union action; countries that make no effort to control their carbon emissions but benefit from collective international action to reduce global warming. The problem in such cases is that it may be rational for individuals, considering only their own self-interest, to free-ride, but if too many people reason in the same way, none of the hoped-for benefits will be achieved. So is it right to use coercion? Is it right to enforce union membership through closed shops, or to push through binding international agreements, backed by threat of sanctions or other force?

Other close relatives of golden-rule delinquents are hypocrites, who take the small step from not doing as they would be done by to not practising what they preach: the adulterous vicar who eulogizes the sanctity of marriage; the politician who takes a backhander while fulminating against financial impropriety. As in violations of the golden rule, the basic objection in these cases is inconsistency: between people's stated opinions and the beliefs that are suggested by their behaviour; between the importance they claim to attach to certain propositions and the indifference that one infers from their actions.

Ideal observers and impartial spectators

The universal appeal of the golden rule – the reason it has featured in some form or other in virtually every philosophical and religious ethical system – is partly due to its sheer generality. Thus, according to particular taste and need, its dominant facets may be variously seen to include (among other things) reciprocity, impartiality and universality. The rule's protean character has also meant that it (or something very like it) has popped up in many different guises in many different systems. One influential incarnation is that of the 'ideal observer'. The assumption here is that our uncorrected or untutored instincts will be distorted by various factors, including ignorance, partiality for friends and lack of sympathy for others. As an antidote to these, an ideal (or idealized) observer is introduced, whose view is unclouded by such flaws and so provides a suitable moral yardstick.

One of the best-known elaborations of this notion is the 'impartial and well-informed spectator' drawn by the Scottish philosopher and economist Adam Smith in his *Theory of the Moral Sentiments* of 1759. Smith's spectator is the voice of conscience within, 'the man within the breast, the great judge and arbiter' of our conduct; whose jurisdiction is founded 'in the desire of possessing those qualities, and performing those actions, which we love and admire in other people; and in the dread of possessing those qualities, and performing those actions, which we hate and despise in other people'.

simplicity, while part of its attraction, makes it an easy target for critical sniping. People take their pleasures in very different ways; the non-masochistic majority should be wary of the masochist who firmly adheres to the golden rule. Yet when we try defining and refining the rule, we risk sapping its force. We may wish to specify the context and circumstances in which the rule is to apply, but if we are too specific, the rule begins to lose the universality that is a large part of its appeal. At the heart of the golden rule is a demand for consistency, but the egoist can consistently pursue her own self-interest and show no inconsistency in recommending that others do likewise.

Rather than seeing the golden rule as a moral panacea (as some have sought to do), it is more fruitful to regard it as an essential ingredient, a necessary part of the foundations of our ethical thinking: a demand not only for consistency, but for fairness; the requirement that you seek imaginatively to put yourself in someone else's position, that you show to others the kind of respect and understanding that you would hope to receive yourself. As such, the golden rule is a useful antidote to the kind of moral myopia that often afflicts people when their own close interests are at stake.

the condensed idea
Do as you would be done by

20 Acts and omissions

The water is already up to the cavers' chests and rising fast. If the rescue team don't act quickly, the eight men will be dead in less than half an hour. But what can the rescuers do? There is no way of getting the men out in time, nor of stemming the flow of water. The only option is to divert the flow into the smaller cave nearby. And that's where the two cavers who got separated from the main party are trapped: perfectly safe and waiting patiently to be brought out. Diverting the flow of water will flood the smaller cave in minutes and the two men inside will drown. So what are the rescuers to do? Sit back and let the eight men die, or save their lives at the cost of their two fellow cavers?

A nasty dilemma and no easy solution. Suppose that there really are only two options: diverting the flow of water, which is a deliberate intervention that causes the death of two people who would otherwise live; and sitting back and doing nothing, which allows eight people to die who could have been saved. Although the latter course is graver in terms of loss of life, many feel that it is worse to act in a way that causes people's death than to allow them to die through inaction. The supposed moral difference between what you do and what you allow to happen – the so-called act–omission doctrine – predictably divides ethical theorists. Those who insist that the moral worth of an action should be judged purely on its consequences typically reject the doctrine; while it usually commends itself to those philosophers who stress the intrinsic propriety of certain kinds of action and our duty to perform them irrespective of their consequences (see page 72).

Playing God

Whatever the strength of our intuitions here, the distinction seems to get shakier the more closely we look at it. Much of its appeal, especially in matters of life and death, plays on our fear that by actively doing something we are 'playing God': deciding who should live and who should die. But in what morally relevant sense is 'sitting back and doing nothing' actually doing nothing? It is as much a decision not to act as it is to act, so it appears that in such cases we have no choice but to play God. Would we take a dimmer view of parents who

The principle of double effect

In morally assessing an action, the agent's intention is generally held to be crucial. Our actions may be blameworthy even if their bad consequences were unintended (they may show negligence, for example), but the same actions are likely to be judged much more harshly if the consequences were intended. Closely related to the act–omission doctrine, the principle of double effect turns on the idea of separating the consequences of an action that were intended from those that were merely foreseen. An action that has both good and bad results may then be morally justified if it was performed with the intention of bringing about the good results, while the bad results were foreseen but not intended. The principle has been brought to bear in cases like these:

- A mother's life is saved by the surgical removal (and so killing) of an unborn foetus: saving the mother's life is intended; killing the foetus is anticipated but not intended.

- Pain-killing drugs are given to terminally ill patients: the intention is to relieve their pain; the unintended but known side-effect is that their lives will be shortened.

- An enemy munitions factory is bombed: the intention is to destroy the factory; the unintended but foreseen consequence (or 'collateral damage') is that many civilians living nearby are killed.

In all these cases the idea of double effect is used to bolster the claim that the actions concerned are morally defensible. The doctrine is often used by thinkers favouring an absolutist or duty-based (deontological) conception of morality in order to explain cases where duties conflict and rights are apparently infringed. The principle stands or falls with the distinction between intention and foresight; whether that distinction can bear the weight that is put upon it has been much debated.

Aquinas on self-defence

Formulation of the principle that later became known as the doctrine of double effect is generally credited to the 13th-century philosopher Thomas Aquinas. In discussing the moral justification for killing in self-defence, he drew distinctions that are remarkably close to those that appear in modern legal definitions. The classic statement of the doctrine appears in Aquinas' *Summa Theologica*:

'Nothing hinders one act from having two effects, only one of which is intended, while the other is beside the intention … the act of self-defence may have two effects, one is the saving of one's life, the other is the slaying of the aggressor. Therefore this act, since one's intention is to save one's own life, is not unlawful, seeing that it is natural to everything to keep itself in being, as far as possible. And yet, though proceeding from a good intention, an act may be rendered unlawful, if it be out of proportion to the end. Wherefore if a man, in self-defence, uses more than necessary violence, it will be unlawful: whereas if he repel force with moderation his defence will be lawful.'

chose to drown their children in the bath or others who decided not to feed them and let them slowly starve to death? Nice distinctions between killing and allowing to die seem grotesque in such cases, and we would be most reluctant to say that the 'omission' was in any sense less reprehensible than the 'act'.

The supposed moral distinction between things done and things allowed to happen is often invoked in ethically sensitive medical areas such as euthanasia. In this case a distinction is usually drawn between active euthanasia, where medical treatment hastens the death of a patient, and passive euthanasia, where death results from withholding treatment. Certainly most legal systems (probably tracking our instincts in this case) choose to recognize this difference, but again it is difficult to see any morally relevant distinction between, say, administering death-inducing drugs (a deliberate doing) and withholding life-prolonging drugs (a deliberate not doing). The legal position is based in part on the notion (mainly religious in origin) of

Enola Gay

What would have happened had the B-29 bomber *Enola Gay* not dropped the first atomic bomb on Hiroshima on 6 August 1945? It is likely that this action, followed by the dropping of a second bomb on Nagasaki three days later, led to a faster end to the Second World War: Japan surrendered on 14 August.

It can be argued that, despite the deliberate act causing horrific loss of life, many more lives were saved as a bloody invasion of Japan was avoided. So was the decision to drop 'the bomb' justified? In President Truman's opinion, 'That was not any decision you had to worry about.'

the sanctity of human life; but in terms of the euthanasia debate at least, this is primarily a concern for human life per se, with little or no regard for its quality or for the preferences of the human whose life it is. The law thus has the bizarre consequence of treating a human in a state of extreme distress or suffering with less consideration than would normally be shown to a pet or a farm animal in similar circumstances.

the condensed idea
To do or not to do?

21 Slippery slopes

The moral high ground is naturally surrounded by hills, and with hills come slopes – plenty of them and treacherous too. In popular debate over a wide range of political and social issues, no spectre is conjured up more often or more eagerly than the slippery slope. The image is apparently so suggestive that it is often introduced with little corroboration and accepted with little demur. And yet, while the move to the slippery slope is not necessarily illicit, it is almost invariably proposed in highly charged and emotive areas, and in many cases the appeal is specious or evasive.

The general form of the slippery-slope argument could hardly be simpler: if you permit practice A (either innocuous or mildly objectionable), then it will lead inevitably to practice Z (obnoxious and highly undesirable). Slippery slopes are detected in a bewildering array of situations. Here are some classic examples:

- Permitting active euthanasia to allow terminally ill people to choose the time of their death will lead inexorably to a climate of guilt in which the elderly agree to 'go quietly', so freeing up space, reducing the burden of care and cost on the young, and so on.
- Allow parents to select the sex of their children, and before long they will expect to pick all sorts of desirable attributes and we will have the nightmare of designer babies.
- Legalizing soft drugs such as cannabis will encourage experimentation with hard drugs, and before we know it the streets will be littered with syringe-crazed junkies.
- Showing leniency to young offenders will spur them on to greater criminal acts, and before long our houses will be under siege from thieving and murderous youths.

One common feature of such arguments is to state that there is a slippery slope from A to Z but to keep quiet about stages B to Y. The most notable absentee is generally the most important – some justification of the alleged inevitability of A leading to Z. Focus is shifted to the horrors of Z, often painted in the most lurid colours, and it is hoped that the lack of any discussion of the merits or otherwise of practice A may pass unnoticed.

> ## Boiling frogs
>
> The dangers of creeping social or political change are sometimes
> illustrated by the legend of the boiling frog. If your aim is to boil
> a frog, you will toil in vain (so the story goes) if you drop it into
> boiling water, as it will promptly hop out; such disappointment can
> be avoided, however, if you place the frog in cold water and bring it
> slowly to the boil. In the same way, amphibian-minded libertarians
> might argue, gradual erosion of our civil liberties may lead to a
> cumulative loss (or 'power grab') that would have been vigorously
> opposed if attempted at a single stroke. The socio-political theory is
> more plausible than the frog theory; the falsity of the latter should
> be assumed, not tested.

In effect, argument is replaced by rhetoric. The wisdom of (say) allowing
parents to choose the sex of their children should be considered on its own
merits, and if it is found objectionable, it should arguably be disallowed. If
that practice is itself found to be innocuous, it may be relevant to consider
the supposed inevitability of its leading to some other practice that is
objectionable. But the case may well be hard to make, as in real life, where
there is a genuine danger of a slippery slope appearing, it is possible to
introduce rules and guidelines to prevent uncontrolled slides down it.

Dominoes, wedges and lines

The slippery slope is not the only hazard to which the popular
moralizer alerts us. The first precarious step onto a slippery slope
often precipitates a downward plunge towards a forest of other verbal
perils, where there is a clatter of falling dominoes, snowballs grow to
monstrous proportions, flood-gates are flung wide open, and every
iceberg has hidden depths.

Just as one falling domino can knock over its neighbour and so
initiate a chain of successive topplings, in the **domino effect** it is
suggested that the occurrence of a particular undesirable event will
trigger a sequence of similar events nearby. Its most notorious
appearance was in 1954, when it inspired the 'domino theory' put
forward by US president Dwight Eisenhower to justify US intervention
in Vietnam. According to this theory, allowing one country to fall into

The camel's nose

A colourful and all-too-rarely used variant of the slippery slope, supposedly based on an Arabic fable, gives a delightful glimpse of the peculiar perils of life under canvas (or goatskin). The dire consequences of 'letting the camel's nose into the tent' – especially as the nose is by no means the most offensive part of a camel – are charmingly captured by the 19th-century American poet Lydia Howard Sigourney:

Once in his shop a workman wrought
With languid hand, and listless thought,
When through the open window's space
Behold! – a Camel thrust his face.
'My nose is cold,' he meekly cried,
'Oh, let me warm it by thy side.'
Since no denial word was said,
In came the nose, – in came the head,
As sure as sermon follows text
The long, excursive neck came next,
And then, as falls the threatening storm
In leap'd the whole ungainly form.
Aghast the owner gazed around,
And on the rude invader frown'd,
Convinc'd as closer still he prest,
There was no room for such a guest,
Yet more astonish'd, heard him say,
'If incommoded, go your way,
For in this place I choose to stay.'
Oh, youthful hearts, to gladness born,
Treat not this Arab lore with scorn.
To evil habit's earliest wile
Lend neither ear, nor glance, nor smile,
Choke the dark fountain ere it flows,
Nor even admit the Camel's Nose.

communist hands would inevitably lead to others in Southeast Asia following suit. In the event, the first domino (Vietnam) did topple, but with the notable exception of Cambodia, the predicted spread of communism throughout the region did not follow; the supposed inevitability in this case proved to be nothing of the kind.

A small crack in stone or wood can be progressively widened by driving in a wedge; in the same way, appealing to the figurative **thin end of the wedge** suggests that a small change in (say) a rule or law may be the beginning of, or excuse for, wholesale reform. The suggestion that the right to trial by jury should be withdrawn in complex fraud cases is regarded by some as the thin end of the wedge, as they suspect that the right will gradually be withdrawn in other (perhaps all) areas. The wedge theorists' suspicion remains mere supposition until supported by evidence that policy-makers tend to exhibit wedge-using behaviour in such circumstances.

The problem in **knowing where to draw the line** usually arises from seeking certain knowledge where such knowledge is not possible – from expecting a degree of precision inappropriate to the context. We might all agree, for instance, that it would be wrong to allow many millions of immigrants to settle in the country each year and yet that it is right to allow some to do so. Where do we draw the line? The fact that there is necessarily a degree of vagueness about a decision or about the context in which it is made does not mean that it cannot or should not be made.

Exactly the same kind of problem has long plagued the debate over abortion, where many agree that a newly conceived embryo and a baby at full term are different, yet struggle (because it is impossible) to pinpoint a precise moment at which the change takes place. This is because the development of the foetus is a gradual process, and any point at which we choose to draw a line will be arbitrary to some extent. But this does not mean that any point is as good (or bad) as another, that no line should be drawn, or that any line that is drawn lacks authority or force.

the condensed idea
If you give them an inch ...

22 **Beyond the call of duty**

On 31 July 1916, during the battle of the Somme in northern France, 26-year-old James Miller, a private in the King's Own Royal Lancaster Regiment, 'was ordered to take an important message under heavy shell and rifle fire and to bring back a reply at all costs. He was compelled to cross the open, and on leaving the trench was shot almost immediately in the back, the bullet coming out through his abdomen. In spite of this, with heroic courage and self-sacrifice, he compressed with his hand the gaping wound in his abdomen, delivered his message, staggered back with the answer and fell at the feet of the officer to whom he delivered it. He gave his life with a supreme devotion to duty.'

An act of heroism?

'We may imagine a squad of soldiers to be practising the throwing of live hand grenades; a grenade slips from the hand of one of them and rolls on the ground near the squad; one of them sacrifices his life by throwing himself on the grenade and protecting his comrades with his own body … If the soldier had not thrown himself on the grenade, would he have failed in his duty? Though clearly he is superior in some way to his comrades, can we possibly say that they failed in their duty by not trying to be the one who sacrificed himself? If he had not done so, could anyone have said to him, "You ought to have thrown yourself on that grenade"?'

This story is told in 'Saints and heroes', an important 1958 paper by the British philosopher J.O. Urmson that has driven much recent philosophical debate over supererogatory acts. Urmson identifies three conditions that must be met for an act to count as supererogatory: it cannot be a matter of (ordinary) duty; it must be praiseworthy; and no blame should attach to its omission. All these criteria are clearly met in the above case, Urmson argues, which therefore qualifies as an act of heroism.

What do we make of this kind of behaviour? The British military authorities during the First World War clearly considered Private Miller's actions exceptional, even at a time when many extraordinary deeds were done daily, as he was awarded the Victoria Cross 'for most conspicuous bravery' (the quotation above is taken from Miller's official citation for the award). If Miller had crawled back into the trench immediately after taking the shot that would soon kill him, we would be hard put to *blame* him, or to say that he had acted *wrongly* or that his action was *immoral*. Like his commanding officers, we are surely more likely to judge that Miller's actions went 'beyond the call of duty' and that they deserve special praise. In short, we are likely to praise him for doing what he did but would not have blamed him had he acted differently.

Supererogatory acts

Our common intuitions apparently sit quite comfortably with this kind of assessment. It seems natural to view morality as a two-tiered affair. On one level, there are things that we are all morally required to do: basic obligations that are a matter of duty and set the minimum standard of ordinary morality. Often these are stated negatively, as obligations that we are wrong not to meet: do not lie, cheat, kill. We are expected to meet them ourselves and expect others to do likewise.

In addition to these ordinary moral duties, there are, at a more elevated level, moral ideals. These are often expressed positively and may be open-ended: thus, while there is an ordinary moral duty not to steal from others, great generosity to others is an ideal that is in principle unlimited. Such an action may go beyond what is required by ordinary morality and falls into a category of so-called 'supererogatory acts' – acts that are praiseworthy to perform but not blameworthy to omit. Supererogatory acts are the province of 'heroes and saints'. Such people may consider these acts to be their duty and blame themselves if they fail to perform them, but this is essentially a *personal* sense of duty and others are not entitled to judge them in this way.

Can good actions be optional?

This category of extraordinary, non-obligatory moral actions is philosophically interesting precisely because of the difficulties that some ethical systems have in accommodating it. Such systems typically form some conception of what is good and then define what is right and what is wrong by reference to this standard. The idea that something is acknowledged to be good and yet is not required may then be hard to explain.

According to utilitarianism, at least in its more straightforward versions (see page 69), an action is good if it increases general utility (for example, happiness) and the best action in any situation is the one that produces most utility. Giving most of your money in charitable donations to developing countries would not usually be regarded as a moral obligation; others might praise you for doing it, but would not feel bad about themselves if they did not follow suit. In other words, charity on such a lavish scale is supererogatory. Yet, looking at it from the utilitarian perspective, if such an action promotes general utility (which it very likely would), how can it not be the required thing to do? Supererogatory acts are problematic for Kantian ethics too. Kant places the highest value on moral agency itself (see page 72). Once this is accepted, how can there be any limit on what is done that may enhance or facilitate that agency?

Conflicts of this kind between ethical theories and our ordinary moral sense are damaging, especially for the former. Radical utilitarians might maintain (and some do) that we should accept the full implications of their theory – in effect, denying that any actions can be supererogatory – and alter our ways of life accordingly. But such extreme reformist proposals, which go against the grain of ordinary morality and mark most of us down as moral failures, are certain to alienate more people than they win over. More often, theorists attempt to explain or play down the apparent conflicts. A common strategy is to appeal to some form of exemption or excuse (for instance, abnormal difficulty or danger) that allows a person not to perform some action that would otherwise be obligatory. If this move gets a given theory off the hook, it certainly does so at a cost. For personal factors are introduced, upsetting the universality that is usually regarded as indispensable in the moral realm (see page 76).

Another approach is to introduce ideas such as the doctrine of double effect and the act–omission distinction (see page 81) to explain how it can be right to follow one path when another, apparently preferable one, is also available. But these ideas are not themselves without difficulty, and in any case many will feel that the plausibility of a theory is diminished if it is heavily burdened with footnotes and other qualifications.

the condensed idea
Should we all be heroes?

23 Is it bad to be unlucky?

Two friends, Bell and Haig, spend the evening together in the pub. At closing time, a pint or two over the limit, both totter to their cars to drive home. Bell gets home without alarm, as he has dozens of times before, slumps into bed, and wakes up the next morning with nothing worse than a mild hangover. Haig – just as experienced and adept at driving after a few drinks – makes sedate progress homewards until his journey is interrupted by a young man suddenly flinging himself into the road in front of him. No time to stop, and the man is killed instantly. Haig is thrown into a police cell and wakes up the next morning with a mild hangover and the certainty of spending years in prison.

What do we make of Bell and Haig's behaviour? The law is in no doubt that the latter's behaviour is very much more culpable: Bell, if caught, might be fined and lose his licence for a time; Haig will almost certainly face a significant custodial sentence. The legal view may well reflect our moral sense in this case. We may feel that one whose irresponsible action causes a death is much more blameworthy than another who drives while (a little) over the legal alcohol limit. And yet the only difference between the two drivers in this case – the young man leaping into the road – was a matter of chance. Both drivers behaved irresponsibly, and one of them was unlucky. So the only factor that apparently explains the graver legal and moral assessment of Haig's behaviour is bad luck – something that is, by definition, outside an agent's control.

Moral luck

This differentiation between the two cases seems to be at odds with a very widely held intuition – the feeling that it is only appropriate to judge things morally to the extent that they are under our control. I will take a dim view of your deliberately throwing coffee over me, but I will be less inclined to blame you if the incident takes place on a train and was caused by the driver suddenly slamming on the brakes. Another way of putting the same point is that two people should not be judged differently unless the differences are due to factors that they can control. If a golfer hits his ball into the crowd and happens to hit and kill a spectator, we would not blame him – if we blame him at all – more than another player who plays a similar shot without hitting anybody (although how the unlucky player feels about *himself* is a very different matter).

But if we transfer this way of thinking to the case of Bell and Haig, it seems that we should judge them the same. So should we judge Bell more harshly because of the harm that his irresponsible behaviour might have caused? Or should we be more lenient in our assessment of Haig, because he was behaving no worse than thousands of others and was just unlucky? Of course, we may decide to stick with our initial judgement – that the two cases should be treated differently on the basis of their different outcomes. But if so, we will have to modify our view on the significance of control: we will be forced to conclude that morality is not immune to chance – that there is something that might paradoxically be called 'moral luck'. It looks as though luck might make you bad after all.

Or is it unlucky to be bad?

The issue of whether there is moral luck – whether moral judgements are determined, in part at least, by chance factors outside our control – has been the subject of much recent philosophical discussion. The debate may seem at its sharpest where the issue is so-called 'resultant luck' – as in cases like Bell and Haig's, where the chance outcome of an action appears to affect our evaluation of it. But other kinds of luck may be involved, and the problem may in fact run much deeper.

Confronted with a Bell/Haig-type case, it is tempting to respond that it is the agents' *intentions* – not the consequences of those intentions – that we should consider when apportioning praise or blame. Bell and Haig have the same intentions (neither intends to kill anyone) and therefore should (arguably) be judged the same. But to what extent do we really have control over our intentions? We form the intentions we form because of the kinds of people we are, but there are innumerable factors (falling under the general description of 'constitutive luck') that shape us as people and that we cannot control. Our character is the product of an enormously complex combination of genetic and environmental factors over which we have little or no control. To what extent should we be judged for actions or intentions that flow naturally from our character? If I can't help being cowardly or selfish – if it is as it were 'in my nature' to be so – is it fair to blame or criticize me for running away from danger or thinking too much of my own interests?

It is possible to keep pushing back the boundaries of luck further and further. If we consider another kind of luck – circumstantial luck – we see the extent to which an evaluation of moral badness may depend on being in the wrong place at the wrong time. Taken to its logical conclusion, the debate over whether there is such a thing as moral luck merges with the issue of free will and raises the same questions: in the final analysis, is *anything* we do done freely, and if there is no freedom, can there be responsibility? And without responsibility, what justification is there for blame and punishment (see page 192)?

Common intuitions on moral luck are far from uniform or consistent. This uncertainty is reflected in a degree of polarization in the philosophical positions adopted on the issue. Some philosophers deny that there is any such thing as moral luck and then try to explain or explain away the manifest appearances of it in our ordinary moral discourse. Others accept that moral luck exists and then go on to consider whether and how far this obliges us to reform or revise the way we make moral assessments. The stakes are high, in terms of the risk of damage to some very basic assumptions about the way we conduct our moral lives; and as yet there is little sign of consensus.

Wrong time, wrong place

We can only display the good and bad points of our characters if circumstances provide us with opportunities to do so: we are all at the mercy of 'circumstantial luck'. You cannot show your great natural generosity if you lack the resources to be generous with or the potential beneficiaries to be generous to. We may think that we would never have displayed the depravity of Nazi guards at Auschwitz, but of course we will never know that for sure. All we can say for certain is that we are very fortunate that we will never have to find out. So was the Nazi guard unfortunate that he was put in a situation where he could find out? Was he unlucky to be bad?

the condensed idea
Does fortune favour the good?

24 Virtue ethics

For most of the last 400 years, moral philosophers have tended to focus primarily on actions, not agents – on what sort of things we should do rather than what sort of people we should be. The main task of the philosopher has been to discover and explain the principles on which this moral obligation is based and to formulate rules that guide us to behave in accordance with these principles.

Very different proposals have been made on the nature of the underlying principles themselves, from the duty-based ethics of Kant to the consequentialist utilitarianism of Bentham and Mill. Nevertheless, at root there has been a shared assumption that the core issue is the justification of actions rather than the character of agents, which has been seen as secondary or merely instrumental. But virtue has not always played handmaiden to duty or some other good beyond itself.

Until the Renaissance and the first stirrings of the scientific revolution, the overwhelmingly important influences in philosophy and science were the great thinkers of classical Greece – Plato and, above all, his pupil Aristotle. For them, the main concern was the nature and cultivation of good character; the principal question was not 'What is the right thing to do (in such and such circumstances)?' but 'What is the best way to live?' Given this very different set of priorities, the nature of virtue, or moral excellence, was of central interest. Aristotle's philosophy was eclipsed for several centuries from the time of Galileo and Newton, when attention shifted the rules and principles of moral conduct. From the middle of the 20th century, however, some thinkers began to express their dissatisfaction with the prevailing trend in moral philosophy and to revive interest in the study of character and virtues. This recent movement in moral theorizing, inspired principally by Aristotle's ethical philosophy, has advanced under the banner of 'virtue ethics'.

The Greeks on virtue
According to Aristotle, as to other Greek thinkers, being a good person and knowing right from wrong is not primarily a matter of understanding and applying certain moral rules and principles.

There is, on the face of it, such a gulf between the task as conceived by Aristotle and the approach adopted by most recent philosophers that some have suggested that the terminology should be adapted to reflect the distinction. It has been proposed that the term 'morality' should be restricted to systems such as that of Kant, where the focus is on principles of duty and rules of conduct; while 'ethics' – which is derived from the Greek word for 'character' – is reserved for more Aristotelian approaches, in which priority is given to the dispositions of the agent and to practical (not just moral) wisdom. There has been disagreement over the usefulness of the distinction, which others regard as setting up a false (because misleadingly sharp) opposition between Aristotle and the philosophers with whom he is contrasted.

Rather, it is a question of being or becoming the kind of person who, by acquiring wisdom through proper practice and training, will habitually behave in appropriate ways in the appropriate circumstances. In short, having the right kind of character and dispositions, natural and acquired, issues in the right kind of behaviour. The dispositions in question are virtues. These are expressions or manifestations of *eudaimonia*, which the Greeks took to be the highest good for man and the ultimate purpose of human activity. Usually translated as 'happiness', *eudaimonia* is actually broader and more dynamic than this, best captured by the idea of 'flourishing' or 'enjoying a good (successful, fortunate) life'. The Greeks often talk about four cardinal virtues – courage, justice, temperance (self-mastery) and intelligence (practical wisdom) – but a pivotal doctrine for both Plato and Aristotle is the so-called 'unity of the virtues'. Founded in part on the observation that a good person must recognize how to respond sensitively to the sometimes conflicting demands of different virtues, they conclude that the virtues are like different facets of a single jewel, so that it is not in fact possible to possess one virtue without having them all. In Aristotle, the possession and cultivation of all the various virtues means that the good man has an overarching virtue,

The golden mean

The golden mean is central to Aristotle's conception of virtue. The doctrine is sometimes mistakenly seen as a call for moderation, in the sense of striking a middle path in all things, but this is far from his meaning. As the quotation makes clear, the mean is to be defined strictly by reference to reason. To take an example: the virtue that lies as a mean between cowardice and rashness is courage. Being courageous is not only a matter of avoiding cowardly actions such as running away from the enemy; it is also necessary to avoid foolhardy, devil-may-care bravado, such as mounting a futile attack that will be damaging to oneself and one's comrades. Courage depends on reason governing one's baser, non-rational instincts: the crucial point is that action should be appropriate to the circumstances, as determined by practical wisdom responding sensitively to the facts of the situation.

'Virtue, then, is a state of character concerned with choice, lying in the mean which is defined by reference to reason. It is a mean between two vices, one of excess and one of deficiency; and again, it is a mean because the vices respectively fall short or exceed what is right in both passions and actions, while virtue both finds and chooses that which is intermediate.'
Aristotle, c.350 BC

usually called 'magnanimity' (from the Latin meaning 'great-souled'). The Aristotelian *megalopsychos* ('great-souled man') is the archetype of goodness and virtue: the man of distinguished station in life and worthy of great things; anxious to confer benefits but reluctant to receive them; showing a proper pride and lacking excessive humility.

The hierarchy implied in the unity of the virtues led Plato to the strong conclusion that the different virtues are in fact one and the same and that they are subsumed under a single virtue – knowledge. The idea that virtue is (identical with) knowledge led Plato to deny the possibility of *akrasia*, or weakness of will: for him, it was impossible to 'know the better yet do the worse'; to behave intemperately, for instance, was not a matter of weakness but of ignorance. The idea that we cannot knowingly do wrong, clearly at odds with experience, was resisted by Aristotle, who was always anxious where possible to avoid diverging from common beliefs (*endoxa*). For Plato and Aristotle, behaving virtuously was inextricably linked to the exercise of reason, or rational choice; and Aristotle elaborated this idea into the influential doctrine of the (golden) mean (see box opposite).

the condensed idea
What you are, not what you do

25 Do animals feel pain?

'**O** my leg!' he cried. 'O my poor shin!' and he sat up on the snow and nursed his leg in both his front paws.

'Poor old Mole!' said the Rat kindly. 'You don't seem to be having much luck today, do you? Let's have a look at the leg.

'Yes,' he went on, going down on his knees to look, 'you've cut your shin, sure enough. Wait until I get at my handkerchief, and I'll tie it up for you.'

'I must have tripped over a hidden branch or a stump,' said the Mole miserably. 'O, my! O, my!'

'It's a very clean cut,' said the Rat, examining it again attentively. 'That was never done by a branch or a stump … '

'Well, never mind what done it,' said the Mole, forgetting his grammar in his pain. 'It hurts just the same, whatever done it.'

Do real animals feel pain, or only fictional ones like the mole in *The Wind in the Willows*? We may be reasonably confident that non-human animals do not talk, but beyond that not much is certain. How we respond to the question of animal pain, and the broader issue of animal consciousness, has a direct bearing on other pressing questions:

- Is it right for tens of millions of rats, mice and even primates, to be used in medical research, product testing, etc.?
- Is it right for moles and other so-called 'pests' to be poisoned, gassed and otherwise exterminated?
- Is it right for billions of animals such as cows and chickens to be slaughtered to provide us with food?

Most philosophers agree that consciousness (especially suffering pain) is critical in deciding what moral consideration we should show to animals. If we agree that even some animals are capable of feeling pain and that causing unnecessary pain is wrong, we must conclude it is wrong to inflict unnecessary pain on them. Unpacking this further – deciding, in particular, what if anything might count as an adequate justification for inflicting pain on animals – then becomes a morally pressing task.

By analogy with our own minds, we may infer broad similarities between the conscious experience of humans and (some) animals, but how far can we move beyond this? The subjective experience of an animal must be intimately tied up with its way of life and the particular environment to which it is evolutionarily adapted; and as Thomas Nagel pointed out, we do not have the faintest idea what it would be *like* to be a bat – or any other animal (see page 32). This problem was made even more acute by the 'linguistic turn' that came to dominate much philosophy of mind in the 20th century. According to this, our mental life is essentially underpinned or mediated by language, and our thoughts are necessarily represented inwardly in linguistic terms. Such a view, rigidly applied to non-linguistic animals, would oblige us to deny that they can entertain any thoughts at all. Attitudes have since softened, and most philosophers would allow that (some) non-human animals have thoughts, albeit of a simple kind.

Inside animal minds

So what do we know about what goes on inside animals' heads? Do animals have feelings, thoughts and beliefs? Are they capable of reasoning? The truth is we know very little about animal consciousness. Our lack of knowledge in this area is really a generalized version of the problem of knowing anything about other *human* minds (see page 44). We cannot, it seems, know for certain that other people experience things in the same way as we do or, indeed, that they experience anything at all, so it is little surprise that we are in no better a situation (and probably considerably worse) with respect to non-human animals.

In the case of both human and animal minds, the best we can do is use an argument from analogy with our own case. Mammals seem to react to pain in much the same way as humans, recoiling from a source of pain, letting out a range of shrieks and screams, and so on. In physiological terms, too, there is a basic uniformity across mammalian nervous systems; and close parallels are likewise found in genetic makeup and evolutionary origin. Given so many similarities, it is plausible to suppose that there should be resemblances at the level of subjective experience too. And the closer the similarities in physiology and other relevant respects, the safer the inference to a similarity in subjective experience.

In this way we seem to be on relatively safe ground in making inferences about our close relatives, apes and monkeys; rather less so when it comes to more distantly related mammals such as rats and moles. The analogy is weaker but still plausible in the case of other vertebrates (birds, reptiles, amphibians and fish) and decidedly precarious when we move to invertebrates (insects, slugs and jellyfish). This is not to say that such animals are not sentient, do not experience pain and so on, but it is highly dubious to base such a claim on an analogy with our own consciousness. The difficulty is to know on what other basis we could possibly ground a claim.

Animal experimentation: is it right and does it work?

The morality of using animals in medical research and product-testing can be looked at in two ways. One is to ask if it is right for us to treat non-human animals purely as a means to further our own ends; whether it is ethical to cause animals to suffer (assuming that they can suffer) and to infringe their rights (assuming that they have rights) in order to improve our health, to test drugs, and so on. This is one aspect of the big question concerning the moral stance that we should adopt towards animals (see page 104). The other consideration is a more practical one. Testing the toxicity of a product on a mouse is only worth doing (assuming that it is ethical to do it at all) if mice and men are sufficiently similar in relevant physiological respects that human conclusions can be drawn from murine data. The problem is that the second, pragmatic consideration encourages the use of higher mammals such as monkeys and apes because they are physiologically closer to humans; but it is precisely the use of such animals that is likely to meet the stiffest opposition on ethical grounds.

the condensed idea
Animal cruelty?

26 Do animals have rights?

Each year in the mid-2000s, throughout the world:
• *approximately 50 million animals are used in scientific research and testing;*
• *over 250 million tonnes of meat are produced;*
• *nearly 200 million tonnes of fish and other aquatic animals are harvested from seas and rivers.*

The figures are approximate (especially for research, much of which is not recorded at all), but it is clear that a vast mountain of animals is used every year in the interests of humans. Rather than 'used', many people – and the number is increasing – would say 'exploited' or 'sacrificed'. For many regard the use of animals for food and research to be morally indefensible and a violation of the animals' basic rights.

The basis of animal rights

What grounds are there for saying that animals have rights? One common argument, essentially utilitarian in character, runs as follows: **1.** animals can feel pain; **2.** the world is a better place if pain is not inflicted unnecessarily; therefore **3.** unnecessary pain should not be inflicted on animals.

The first premise has been subject to much recent debate (see page 100). It seems highly implausible to suppose that animals such as apes and monkeys, which resemble us in many relevant respects, do not have the capacity to feel something very similar to the pain that we feel. However, it seems just as unlikely that animals such as sponges and jellyfish, which have very simple nervous systems, feel anything remotely like human pain. The difficulty then becomes where to draw the line, and – as is often the case when it comes to drawing lines (see page 87) – it is hard to avoid a strong whiff of arbitrariness. We may settle for a qualified '*Some* animals can feel pain', but a troubling question mark hangs over the actual scope.

The second premise may seem largely unimpeachable (*pace* the odd masochist), but again there is a danger that it becomes qualified to the point of vacuity. Some have tried to undermine the claim by drawing a distinction between pain and suffering. The latter, it is alleged, is a complex emotion involving both recollection of past pain and anticipation of pain to come, while pain in itself is no more than a fleeting sensation of the present; it is suffering that counts when it comes to moral consideration, but animals (or some animals) are only capable of feeling pain. Even if we allow such a distinction, however, it seems unreasonable to claim that pain is still not a bad thing, even if suffering is worse.

Much more problematic is the 'unnecessarily' part of the second premise. For there is nothing to stop an opponent arguing that some degree of animal pain is a price worth paying for human benefits in terms of improved health, enhanced product safety, and so on. Being utilitarian, the argument apparently calls for some kind of calculus of pain, trading animal pain against human benefit; but the required calculation – difficult enough even if only human pain were involved – looks utterly intractable when animal pain is added to the equation.

This assault on the premises inevitably damages the conclusion. Uncharitably, we might say that it comes to no more than the claim that we should not cause pain to some (perhaps very few) animals unless doing so brings some (perhaps minimal) benefit to humans. On this view, 'animal rights' boil down to (arguably) the right of a small number of animals not to have pain inflicted on them unless doing so brings a small benefit to humans.

Are rights right?

This is not a conclusion that any serious advocate of animal rights could be happy with. More robust and sophisticated justifications than the version outlined above have been offered, all aiming to deliver a less enervated conception of what kind of rights animals might enjoy. While the Australian philosopher Peter Singer has been the champion of a utilitarian approach to the issue, a deontological line advocated by the American Tom Regan has also been highly influential. According to Regan, animals – or at least animals above a certain level of complexity – are 'subjects of a life'; it is this fact that confers on them certain basic rights, which are violated when an animal is treated as a source of meat or a human proxy in experimentation or product-testing. In this way animal rights are spared the kind of cost–benefit analysis that can be so damaging to a utilitarian view.

Speciesism

Most people don't keep other people in filthy cramped conditions and then eat them; or test chemicals with unknown properties on children; or genetically modify humans in order to study their biology. Are there grounds for treating animals in these ways? There must (proponents of animal rights argue) be some morally relevant justification for refusing to give animals' interests equal consideration to those of humans. Otherwise it is a matter of mere prejudice or bigotry – discrimination on the basis of species, or 'speciesism': a basic lack of respect for the dignity and needs of animals other than humans, no more defensible than discrimination on the basis of gender or race.

Is it obviously wrong to favour our own species? Lions, for instance, are generally more considerate towards other lions than they are towards warthogs; so why shouldn't humans show a similar partiality? Many reasons have been suggested why they should:

- humans have a higher level of intelligence than animals (or at least the potential to do so);

- predation is natural (animals in nature eat other animals);

- animals are specially bred to be eaten/used in experiments (and wouldn't exist otherwise);

- we need to eat meat (although millions of apparently healthy people don't);

- animals lack souls (but are we certain that humans have them?).

It is easy to counter these justifications and, in general, it is difficult to frame criteria that neatly encompass all humans and exclude all animals. For instance, if we decide it is superior intellect that counts, would we use this criterion to justify using a child or mentally retarded person with a level of intelligence below that of a chimpanzee in a scientific experiment? Or if we decide it is 'nature's way', we soon find there are many things that animals (including humans) naturally do that we might not wish to encourage: sometimes male lions follow their nature in killing a rival's offspring, but such behaviour would generally be frowned upon in humans.

The difficulties in sustaining a conception of animal rights on a par with human rights are considerable, and some philosophers have questioned whether it is appropriate or helpful to introduce the notion of rights at all. It is usually supposed that rights impose duties or obligations on their bearers; that talk of rights presupposes some kind of reciprocity – the kind that could never actually exist between humans and animals. There is a real issue at stake, it is argued – the proper and humane treatment of animals – which is obscured by being provocatively dressed up in the language of rights.

the condensed idea
Human wrongs?

27 Forms of argument

Arguments are the bricks from which philosophical theories are constructed; logic is the straw that binds those bricks together. Good ideas are worth little unless they are supported by good arguments – they need to be rationally justified, and this cannot be done properly without firm and rigorous logical under-pinning. Clearly presented arguments are open to assessment and criticism, and it is this continual process of reaction, revision and rejection that drives philosophical progress.

An argument is a rationally sanctioned move from accepted foundations (*premises*) to a point that is to be proved or demonstrated (the *conclusion*). The premises are the basic propositions that must be accepted, provisionally at least, so that an argument can get underway. The premises themselves may be established in several ways, as a matter of logic or on the basis of evidence (that is, empirically), or they may be the conclusions of previous arguments; but in any case the premises must be supported independently of the conclusion in order to avoid circularity. The move from premises to conclusion is a matter of *inference*, the strength of which determines the robustness of the argument. The business of distinguishing good inferences from bad is the central task of logic.

The role of logic

Logic is the science of analysing argument and of establishing principles or foundations on which sound inferences can be made. As such its concern is not with the particular content of arguments but with their general structure and form.

So, given an argument such as 'All birds are feathered; the robin is a bird; therefore the robin is feathered', the logician abstracts the form 'All *F*s are *G*; *a* is an *F*; so *a* is *G*', in which the particular terms are replaced by symbols and the strength of the inference can be determined independently of the subject matter. The study of logic formerly focused primarily on simple inferences of this kind (called *syllogisms*), but since the beginning of the 20th century it has been transformed into a highly subtle and sophisticated analytical tool.

Deduction

The example given above ('All birds are feathered …') is *a deductive* argument. In this case the conclusion follows from (is entailed by) the premises, and the argument is said to be 'valid'. If the premises of a valid argument are true, the conclusion is guaranteed to be true, and the argument is said to be 'sound'. The conclusion of a deductive argument is implicit in its premises; in other words, the conclusion does not 'go beyond' its premises or say any more than is already implied by them. Another way of putting this, which reveals the argument's underlying logical character, is that you cannot accept the premises and deny the conclusion without contradicting yourself.

Induction

The other main way of moving from premises to conclusion is induction. In a typical *inductive* argument, a general law or principle is inferred from particular observations of how things are in the world. For instance, from a number of observations that mammals give birth to live young, it might be inferred, inductively, that all mammals do so. Such an argument can never be valid (in the sense that a deductive argument can) in that its conclusion does not follow *necessarily* from its premises; in other words, it is possible for the premises to be true but the conclusion false (as it is in the example given, where the conclusion is shown to be false by the existence of egg-laying mammals such as the platypus). This is because inductive reasoning always moves beyond its premises, which never *entail* a given conclusion but only support it or make it probable to some degree. So inductive arguments are generalizations or extrapolations of various kinds: from the particular to the general; from the observed to the unobserved; from past and present events or states of affairs to future ones.

Inductive reasoning is ubiquitous and indispensable. It would be impossible to live our everyday lives without using observed patterns and continuities in the past and present to make predictions about how things will be in the future. Indeed, the laws and assumptions of science are often held to be paradigmatic cases of induction (see page 132). But are we justified in drawing such inferences? The Scottish philosopher David Hume thought that we are not – that there is no

Paradox or fallacy?

'The prisoner will be hanged at dawn, by next Saturday at the latest, and will not know in advance the day on which the sentence is to be carried out.' It sounds bad, but the wily prisoner has a comforting train of thought. 'The hanging can't be on Saturday because I would know that in advance if I were still alive on Friday. So the latest day it can be is the Friday. But it can't be then, because I would know that if I were still alive on the Thursday ... ' And so he works his way back through all the days to the present and is relieved to discover that the execution cannot take place. So it comes as a bit of a shock to the prisoner when he is in fact hanged on the following Tuesday.

Paradox or fallacy? Well, perhaps both. The story (known as the prediction paradox) is paradoxical because an apparently impeccable line of reasoning gives rise to a conclusion that is manifestly false, as the rueful prisoner discovers. Paradoxes typically involve seemingly sound arguments that lead to apparently contradictory or otherwise unacceptable conclusions. Sometimes there is no way of avoiding the conclusion, and this may call for re-examination of various attendant beliefs and assumptions; or some fallacy (error of reasoning) may be spotted in the argument itself. Either way, paradoxes demand philosophical attention because they invariably point to confusions or inconsistencies in our concepts and reasoning.

Some of the most famous paradoxes (several of which are discussed in the following pages) have been amazingly resistant to solution and continue to perplex philosophers.

rational basis for our reliance on induction. Inductive reasoning, he argued, presupposes a belief in the 'uniformity of nature', according to which it is assumed that the future will resemble the past when relevantly similar conditions obtain. But what possible grounds could there be for such an assumption, except inductive ones? And if the supposed uniformity of nature can only be justified in this way, it cannot itself – without circularity – be used in defence of induction.

In a similar vein, some have tried to justify induction on the basis of its past successes: basically, it works. But the supposition that it will continue to work in the future can only be inferred *inductively* from its past successes, so the argument cannot get off the ground. In Hume's own view, we cannot help but reason inductively (and indeed he does not suggest that we shouldn't reason in this way), but he insists that our doing so is a matter of custom and habit and is not rationally justified . The so-called 'problem of induction' that Hume left behind, especially as it impacts upon the foundations of science, remains an area of active debate to this day.

the condensed idea
Infallible reasoning?

28 The barber paradox

n a village there lives a barber who shaves all and only the people who do not shave themselves. So who shaves the barber? If he shaves himself, he does not; if he does not shave himself, he does.

On the face of it, the puzzle at the centre of the barber paradox may not seem too hard to fathom. A scenario that at first glance looks plausible quickly collapses into contradiction. The innocent-looking job description (a man 'who shaves all and only the people who do not shave themselves') is in fact logically impossible, since the barber cannot, without contradicting the description of himself, belong either to the group who shave themselves or to the group who do not. A man fitting the description of the barber cannot (logically) exist. So there is no such barber: paradox solved.

> 'A scientist can hardly meet with anything more undesirable than to have the foundation give way just as the work is finished. In this position I was put by a letter from Mr Bertrand Russell as the work was nearly through the press'
>
> Gottlob Frege, 1903

The significance of the barber paradox in fact lies not in its content but in its form. Structurally, this paradox is similar to another, more important problem known as Russell's paradox, which concerns not clean-shaven villagers but mathematical sets and their contents. This related paradox has proved a great deal less easy to solve; indeed, it is no exaggeration to say that, a century ago, it was largely responsible for undermining the very foundations of mathematics.

Russell and set theory

The idea of sets is fundamental to mathematics, because they are the purest objects under its scrutiny. The mathematical method involves defining groups (sets) of elements that satisfy certain criteria, such as the set of all real numbers greater than 1 or the set of prime numbers; operations are then performed so that further properties can be deduced about the elements contained within the set or sets concerned. From a philosophical perspective, sets have been of particular interest because the recognition that all of mathematics (numbers, relations, functions) could

'This sentence is false'

The problem of self-reference that lies at the heart of the barber paradox and Russell's paradox is shared by a number of other well-known philosophical puzzles. Perhaps most famous of all is the so-called 'liar paradox', the supposed origins of which go back to the 7th century BC, when the Greek Epimenides – a Cretan himself – is alleged to have said 'All Cretans are liars'. The simplest version is the sentence 'This sentence is false', which if true is false and if false is true. The paradox can be captured in a pair of sentences: on one side of a piece of paper – 'The sentence on the other side is false'; on the other – 'The sentence on the other side is true'. In this formulation each sentence on its own is apparently unexceptionable, so it is hard to dismiss the paradox as simply meaningless, as some have suggested.

Another interesting variant is Grelling's paradox. This involves the notion of autological words (words that describe themselves), for example, 'pentasyllabic', which itself has five syllables; and heterological words (words that do not describe themselves), for example, 'long', which is itself short. Every word must be of one kind or the other, so now consider: is the word 'heterological' itself heterological? If it is, it is not; if it is not, it is. There's no escape from the barber's shop, it seems.

be exhaustively formulated within set theory fuelled the ambition of using sets to ground mathematics on purely logical foundations.

At the beginning of the 20th century the German mathematician Gottlob Frege was attempting to define the whole of arithmetic in logical terms by means of set theory. At this time it was assumed that there were no restrictions on the conditions that could be used to define sets. The problem, recognized by the British philosopher Bertrand Russell in 1901, centred on the question of self-membership of set. Some sets have themselves as members: for instance, the set of mathematical objects is itself a mathematical object. Others do not: the set of prime numbers is not itself a prime number. Now consider the set of all sets that are not members of themselves. Is this set a

Philosophical arguments are often complex and have to be expressed with great precision. Sometimes, philosophers get a little carried away by the majesty of their own intellect and trying to follow their arguments can feel like wading through treacle. If you thought the rules of cricket were hard to follow, see if you can keep up with Bertrand Russell's reasoning as he defines 'the number of a class'.

'This method is, to define as the number of a class the class of all classes similar to the given class. Membership of this class of classes (considered as a predicate) is a common property of all the similar classes and of no others; moreover every class of the set of similar classes has to the set a relation which it has to nothing else, and which every class has to its own set. Thus the conditions are completely fulfilled by this class of classes, and it has the merit of being determinate when a class is given, and of being different for two classes which are not similar. This, then, is an irreproachable definition of the number of a class in purely logical terms.'

member of itself? If it is, it isn't; and if it isn't, it is. In other words, membership of this set depends on not being a member of the set. A straight contradiction, and hence the (barber-like) paradox. However, in contrast to the barber case, it is not possible simply to jettison the offending set – not, at any rate, without blowing a hole in set theory as it was then understood.

> **'The point of philosophy is to start with something so simple as not to seem worth stating, and to end with something so paradoxical that no one will believe it.'**
> Bertrand Russell, 1918

The existence of contradictions at the heart of set theory, exposed by Russell's paradox, showed that the mathematical definition and treatment of sets was fundamentally flawed. Given that any statement can (logically) be proved on the basis of a contradiction, it followed – disastrously – that any and every proof, while not necessarily invalid, could not be known to be valid.

Mathematics basically had to be rebuilt from the foundations. The key to the solution lay in the introduction of appropriate restrictions on the principles governing set membership. Russell not only exposed the problem but was one of the first to attempt a solution, and while his own attempt was only partially successful, he helped to set others on the right path.

the condensed idea
If it is, it isn't; if it isn't, it is

29 The gambler's fallacy

Minds racing, Monty and Carlo gawped at the croupier as she began to rake in the losing chips. Neither had placed a bet over the last few spins, preferring to get a feel for the way the table was playing. But they had been growing steadily impatient as red numbers had come up time after time – five times in a row now; they could wait no longer. 'You've got to be in it to win it', they both thought, not with total originality …

… As they reached over to place their chips, Monty thought:
'Five reds in a row! Couldn't be six. What would be the chances against that? By the law of averages it's got to be black.'
At the same moment, Carlo thought:
'Wow, reds are red hot! I'm not missing out this time. It's got to be red.'
'Rien ne va plus … No more bets', called the croupier.

Can't beat the house

Casino games typically have some kind of a 'house edge', meaning that the odds are stacked slightly in favour of the bank. For instance, in roulette, there are one (European) or two (US) slots that are neither red nor black, so that the chances of winning on a red or black number is slightly less than 1 in 2. Likewise in pontoon (*vingt-et-un*), you have to *beat* the bank: the bank's 21 beats the player's 21. While it is always possible for a single player to beat the house, overall and over time it is almost inevitable that the house will come out on top.

So who is more likely to win, Monty or Carlo? The answer is perhaps Carlo and probably neither. What is certain is that both of them – in common with perhaps billions of real people throughout history (dice have been found dating back to around 2750 BC – are guilty of the so-called gambler's (or Monte Carlo) fallacy.

'Black must be due'

Monty is right that five reds in a row is unusual: the probability (on a fair table and ignoring the one or two green zero slots; see box opposite) is 1 in 32; and the chances of six in a row are even lower – 1 in 64. But these odds apply only at the *beginning* of the sequence, before there have been any spins of the wheel. The problem for Monty is that this relatively rare event (five reds in a row) has *already happened* and has no bearing whatsoever on whether the next number is red;

> 'I feel like a fugitive from the law of averages.'
> Bill Mauldin, 1945

If you're in a lottery, start digging ...

What are the chances of the same six numbers coming up twice in a row in the UK national lottery? About 1 in 200,000,000,000,000 (200 million million). Not great odds, so you would have to be a real mug to choose last week's numbers again ... Well perhaps, but no more of a mug than if you chose any other six numbers. It is just another case of the gambler's fallacy: once a given set of numbers has *already come up*, the chances of those numbers coming up again are no better or worse than any other selection – a much more tempting 14 million to 1. So, for people wondering if the best strategy is to stick with one set of numbers or change them each week, there's no difference – but even better is to dig a hole in the garden and look for buried treasure.

The law of averages

The 'law of averages' is often invoked in support of the gambler's fallacious thinking. This claims, roughly, that something is more likely to occur in the future because it has occurred less frequently than expected in the past (or, conversely, it is less likely to occur in the future because it occurred more frequently in the past). On this basis it is supposed that things will 'even themselves out in the long run'.

The attraction of this bogus law is due in part to its similarity to a genuine statistical law – the law of large numbers. According to this, if you toss an unbiased coin a small number of times, say 10 times, the occurrence of heads may deviate considerably from the mean (average), which is 5; but if you toss it a large number of times – say 1,000 times – the occurrence of heads is likely to be much closer to the mean (500). And the bigger the number of tosses, the closer it is likely to be. So, in a series of random events of equal probability, it is true that things will even themselves out if the series is extended far enough. However, this statistical law has no bearing on the probability of any single event occurring; in particular, a current event has no recollection of any previous deviation from the mean and cannot alter its outcome to correct an earlier imbalance. So there is no comfort here for the gambler.

The error of reasoning seen in the gambler's fallacy is nicely illustrated by the story of the man who was caught carrying a bomb on to a plane. 'The chances of there being one bomb on a plane are pretty slim,' he explained to the police. 'So just think how unlikely it is that there would be two!'

the probability of this is, as ever, 1 in 2, or 50:50. Roulette wheels – like coins and dice and lottery balls – do not have memories, so they cannot take account of what has happened in the past in order to balance or even things up: the improbability of any past event or sequence of events (provided they are random and independent) has nothing at all to do with the probability of a future event. To be drawn into supposing otherwise is the gambler's fallacy.

'Red is hot!'

So does Carlo fare any better? Probably not. Like Monty, he has tried to predict a future outcome on the basis of events that apparently have no bearing on it. And if the earlier events are indeed random, he too is a victim of the gambler's fallacy. But this fallacy relates only to outcomes that are genuinely independent. If a horse, say, wins four races in a row, that may be very good evidence that it will win a fifth. If a coin comes up heads 20 times in a row, it may be more plausible to infer that the coin is biased rather than that such an improbable event has happened purely by chance. In the same way, a sequence of four reds *could* indicate that the wheel is biased or rigged. However, while this is not impossible, four reds in a row is hardly uncommon and certainly insufficient on its own to warrant any such conclusion. In the absence of any other evidence, Carlo is no less a dupe than Monty.

the condensed idea
Against the odds

30 The sorites paradox

Suppose (if you have to suppose) that you have a full head of hair. That means that you probably have around 100,000 individual hairs. Now pull one of them out. Does that make you bald? Of course not. A single hair doesn't make any difference. With 99,999 you still have a full head of hair.

Indeed, we would surely all agree that, if you are not bald, removing just one hair could never make you so. And yet, if you pull out another hair, and another, and another … Eventually, if you carry on long enough, you will have none left and you will indubitably be bald. So you apparently move from a state of unquestionable non-baldness to a state of unquestionable baldness by taking a series of steps that can never on their own have that effect. So when did the change come about? This is a version of a famous puzzle, usually attributed to the ancient Greek logician Eubulides of Miletus, known as the sorites paradox. 'Sorites' comes from the Greek word *soros*, meaning a 'heap', as the original formulation of the puzzle features a heap of sand. Expressed in terms of addition (of sand grains) rather than subtraction (of hairs), the argument looks like this:

1 grain of sand does not make a heap.
If 1 grain does not make a heap, then 2 grains do not.
If 2 grains do not make a heap, then 3 grains do not.
[and so on until …]
If 99,999 grains do not make a heap, then 100,000 grains do not.
So 100,000 grains of sand do not make a heap.
But everybody would surely baulk at this conclusion. So what can have gone wrong?

Problems of vagueness

Faced with an unpalatable conclusion of this kind, it is necessary to track back over the argument by which it has been reached. There must be something wrong with the premises on which the argument is based or some error in the reasoning. In fact, in spite of its great antiquity, there is still no clear consensus on how best to tackle this paradox, and various approaches have been taken.

One way out of the paradox is to insist, as some have done, that there is a point at which adding a grain of sand makes a difference; that there is a precise number of grains of sand that marks the boundary between a heap and a non-heap. If there is such a boundary, clearly we do not know where it is, and any proposed dividing line sounds hopelessly arbitrary: do 1,001 grains, say, make a heap, but not 999? This really is a big slap in the face for common sense and our shared intuitions. More promising is to take a closer look at a major assumption underlying the argument: the idea that the process of construction by which a non-heap becomes a heap can be fully and reductively analysed into a series of discrete grain additions. Clearly there are a number of such discrete steps, but equally clearly it seems that these steps are not fully constitutive of the overall process of heap-building.

This faulty analysis fails to recognize that the transition from non-heap to heap is a continuum, and hence that there is no precise point at which the change can be said to occur (for similar problems concerning vagueness, see page 87). This in turn tells us something about the whole class of terms to which the sorites paradox can be applied: not only heap and bald, but also tall, big, rich, fat and countless others. All of these terms are essentially vague, with no clear dividing line separating them from their opposites – short, small, poor, thin, and so on.

One important consequence of this is that there are always borderline cases where the terms do not clearly apply. So, for instance,

Terminal logic

Smokers with ostrich-like tendencies are often susceptible to the kind of faulty reasoning that underlies the sorites paradox. The smoker reasons, not implausibly, that 'the next one won't kill me'. Having established this, he moves by an effortless soritic progression to the claim that 'the one after the next one won't kill me'. And so on, but sadly not ad infinitum. The probable truth that no single cigarette will kill you (though the sum of cigarettes smoked very likely will) represents a pyrrhic victory for the late smoker.

Fuzzy logic

Traditional logic is bivalent, which means that only two truth values are allowed: every proposition must be either true or false. But the inherent vagueness of many terms, apparent in the sorites paradox, suggests that this requirement is too rigid if logic is to encompass the full scope and complexity of natural language.

Fuzzy logic has been developed, initially by the computer scientist Lotfi Zadeh, to allow for imprecision and degrees of truth. Truth is presented as a continuum between true (1) and false (0). So, for instance, a particular proposition that is 'partly true' or 'more or less true' might be represented as true to degree 0.8 and false to degree 0.2. Fuzzy logic has been particularly important in AI (artificial intelligence) research, where 'intelligent' control systems need to be responsive to the imprecisions and nuances of natural language.

while there may be some people who are clearly bald and others who are clearly not, there are many in between who might, according to context and circumstances, be designated as one or the other. This inherent vagueness means that it is not always appropriate to say of a sentence such as 'X is bald' that it is (unequivocally) true or false; rather, there are degrees of truth. This at once creates a tension between these vague terms that occur in natural language and classical logic, which is *bivalent* (meaning that every proposition must be either true or false).

The concept of vagueness suggests that classical logic must be overhauled if it is to fully capture the nuances of natural language. For this reason there has been a move towards the development of fuzzy and other multivalued logics (see box opposite).

the condensed idea
How many grains make a heap?

31 The king of France is bald

Suppose I tell you 'The king of France is bald'. I may sound mad, or perhaps just very badly informed. But is what I say actually false? If it is false, that should mean (according to an established law of logic) that the opposite – 'The king of France is not bald' – is true. And that doesn't sound much better. Or maybe these claims are neither true nor false – they are both just plain nonsense. And yet, while they may be odd things to say, they don't seem to be meaningless.

Do philosophers really trouble themselves over such matters? A sad case, you might think, of inventing an itch to have something to scratch. Well, yes they do: over the last hundred years much high-powered philosophical brain work has been given to the king of France, despite the country having been a republic for more than two centuries. Concerns over this puzzle and others like it provided the inspiration for the British philosopher Bertrand Russell's theory of descriptions, first proposed in an influential 1905 paper named 'On Denoting'. This theory, amongst much other work done by English-speaking philosophers in the early 20th century, was founded on the belief that painstaking analysis of language and its underlying logic is the surest route – perhaps the only route – to knowledge of the world that can be described using that language.

Two thorny matters

The main focus of Russell's theory of descriptions is a category of linguistic terms called definite descriptions: 'the first man on the Moon'; 'the smallest prime number'; 'the world's tallest mountain'; 'the present queen of England'. In terms of grammatical form, the kind of sentence in which such phrases occur – for instance, 'The first man on the Moon was American' – are similar to so-called 'subject–predicate sentences', such as 'Neil Armstrong was American'. In the latter example, 'Neil Armstrong' is a proper noun, which is referential in the sense that it refers to, or denotes, a specific object (in this case a particular human being) and then ascribes some property to it (in this case, the property of being American). In spite of their superficial resemblance to proper nouns, there are a number of problems that arise from treating definite descriptions as if they were referring phrases.

Providing solutions to these puzzles was one of the main motivations behind Russell's 1905 paper. Two of the main problems facing Russell were as follows:

1. Informative identity statements

If *a* and *b* are identical, any property of *a* is a property of *b*, and *a* can be substituted for *b* in any sentence containing the latter without affecting its truth or falsehood. Now George IV wished to know if Scott was the author of *Waverley*. Since Scott was indeed the author of this novel, we can substitute 'Scott' for 'the author of *Waverley*' and so discover that George IV wished to know if Scott was Scott. But this does not appear to be what he wished to know at all. 'Scott is the author of Waverley' is informative in a way that 'Scott is Scott' is not.

2. Preserving the laws of logic

According to the *law of the excluded middle* (a law of classical logic), if '*A* is *B*' is false, '*A* is not *B*' must be true. So, if the statement 'The king of France is bald' is false (as it appears to be, if uttered in the 21st century), 'The king of France is not bald' must be true. But this appears to be false too. If a statement and its negation are both false, logic seems to be fatally undermined.

Russell's solution

The solution to each of these puzzles, in Russell's view, is simply to stop treating the definite descriptions involved as if they were referring expressions in disguise. Appearances in such cases are deceptive: although the various example sentences given above have the *grammatical* form of subject–predicate sentences, they do not have their *logical* form; and it is the logical structure that should determine whether the sentences are true or false and justify any inferences that we may draw from them. Abandoning the referential subject–predicate model, Russell proposes instead that sentences containing definite descriptions should be treated as 'existentially quantified' sentences. So, according to his analysis, a sentence of the general form 'The *F* is *G*' can be split into three separate claims: 'There is an *F*'; 'no more than one thing is the *F*'; and 'if anything is an *F*, then it is *G*.' Using this kind of analysis, Russell swiftly dispels the various mysteries surrounding the crowned heads of Europe:

Existential angst

Many definite descriptions fail to denote *anything*. So, for instance, we might wish to say: 'The highest prime number *does not exist.*' But it is clearly absurd to say of something that it does not exist. That looks like saying that something that exists does not exist – a plain contradiction. Russell's re-analysis of such sentences explains how such non-denoting expressions are meaningful without forcing us to take on unwelcome metaphysical baggage such as non-existent entities. The most contentious piece of (possible) baggage is of course God; the obvious shortcomings of one of the most significant arguments for God's existence (the ontological argument; see page 160) are exposed by a Russellian analysis.

1. 'Scott is the author of *Waverley* is analysed as 'There is an entity, and only one entity, that is the author of *Waverley*, and that entity is Scott'. Clearly it is one thing for George IV to wonder if this is true; quite another for him to wonder about the bland identity statement implied by the referential model.

2. 'The present king of France is bald', in Russell's analysis, becomes 'There is an entity such that it alone is now the king of France, and that one entity is bald'; this is false. The denial of this is not that the king of France is *not* bald (which is also false), but that 'There is *not* an entity such that it alone is now the king of France, and that entity is bald'. This statement is true, so the law of the excluded middle is preserved.

the condensed idea
Language and logic

32 The beetle in the box

'**S**uppose everyone had a box with something in it: we call it a "beetle". No one can look into anyone else's box, and everyone says he knows what a beetle is only by looking at his beetle. – Here it would be quite possible for everyone to have something different in his box. One might even imagine such a thing constantly changing. – But suppose the word "beetle" had a use in these people's language? – If so it would not be used as the name of a thing. The thing in the box has no place in the language-game at all; not even as a *something*: for the box might even be empty … it cancels out, whatever it is.'

What do you mean when you say 'pain'? That's obvious, you might think: you are referring to a particular sensation, to one among many things in your subjective experience. But the Austrian philosopher Ludwig Wittgenstein claims that this is not – indeed *cannot* – be what you are doing. He attempts to explain why by means of the analogy of the beetle in the box. Think of your inner experience as a box; whatever is in the box you call a 'beetle'. Everyone has a box, but they can only ever look into their own, never into anyone else's. Everybody will use the word 'beetle' when talking about the contents of their box, yet it is perfectly possible that the various boxes contain different things or indeed nothing at all. By 'beetle' people will simply mean 'whatever is in their box', and the actual contents will be irrelevant and have nothing to do with the meaning; the beetle itself, whatever it may be, 'drops out of consideration'. When we talk about what is going on inside us we use language that is learned through *public* discourse and is governed by *public* rules. Inner, private sensations, which are beyond scrutiny by others, can play no part in this essentially public activity; whatever these sensations actually are, they have nothing to do with the *meaning* of words like pain.

The private language argument

The beetle-in-the-box analogy is introduced by Wittgenstein at the end of one of the most influential philosophical arguments of the 20th century: the so-called 'private language argument'. Before Wittgenstein a common (and commonsense) view of language was that words get their meaning by representing or standing for things in the world; words are 'denotative' – they are basically names or labels that designate things by being attached to them. In the case of sensations such as pain (so the theory goes), the labelling process happens by some form of introspection, in which a particular mental event or experience is identified and associated with a particular word. Furthermore, for philosophers such as Descartes and Locke who followed the 'way of ideas' (see page 12), according to which *all* our contact with the world is mediated by inner representations or 'ideas', the meaning of *all* language must ultimately be dependent on an inner process in which every word is matched up with some or other mental object. The point of the private language argument is to deny that words could ever get their meaning in this way.

Suppose (Wittgenstein invites us to imagine) that you decide to record every occurrence of a particular sensation by writing in a diary the letter S, where S is a purely private sign meaning 'this sensation I am having now'. How can you tell on a subsequent occasion whether you have applied the sign correctly? The only thing that made the designation right the first time was your decision that it should be so; but the only thing that makes it right on a subsequent occasion is the decision you make at that time. In other words, you can decide what you like: if the designation *seems* right, it is right; and 'that only means that here we can't talk about "right"'. There is no independent 'criterion of correctness', Wittgenstein concludes, nothing outside one's private, subjective experience to act as a standard; it is like someone protesting 'But I know how tall I am!' and laying his hand on top of his head to prove it'. Since there is no non-arbitrary way of telling whether a private sign has been applied correctly or not, such a sign can have no meaning; and a language made up of such signs (a 'private language') would be meaningless, unintelligible even to its own speaker.

Meaning through use

So words do not, and cannot, get their meaning in the way that the 'inner process' model supposes. So how do they get their meaning? Naturally enough, having demonstrated the impossibility of private language, Wittgenstein insists on the necessity of *public* language – that words have meaning 'only in the stream of life'. Far from being

Helping the fly out of the bottle

The repercussions of Wittgenstein's private language argument spread far beyond the philosophy of language. In the first half of the 20th century, language was the focus of much philosophical work, as it was widely assumed that the limits of knowledge were circumscribed by language: 'Whereof one cannot speak, thereof one must be silent', as the young Wittgenstein put it. So a major shift in the understanding of language gave a severe jolt to philosophy as a whole. Just as significant, however, was the impact of Wittgenstein's work on the style and method of philosophy.

Wittgenstein felt that much of modern philosophy was essentially misconceived, based on a fundamental misunderstanding of language – the erroneous thinking exposed by the private language argument. Philosophers, he thought, attach too much importance to particular forms of expression, not enough to the use of language in real social interaction. They become habituated to abstracting and generalizing in order to isolate perceived problems, which they then attempt to solve; in effect they make problems for themselves, all because 'language goes on holiday'. Famously, Wittgenstein's advice was to seek therapy (through philosophy), not theory. Philosophers, in his colourful image, were like flies caught in a bottle; his job was to 'shew the fly the way out of the fly-bottle'.

some mysterious process hidden within us, the meaning of language instead lies at the surface, in the detail of the use to which we put it.

The mistake is to suppose that we should discover the use and purpose of language and *then* probe deeper to unearth – as an additional fact – its meaning. Meaning is something that is established *between* language users: agreement on the meaning of a word is essentially agreement on its application. Language is public, woven seamlessly into the fabric of lives that people live together; to share a language is to share a culture of beliefs and assumptions and to share a common outlook on the world.

To elaborate his idea of meaning as use, Wittgenstein introduces the notion of a 'language game'. Mastery of language resides in being able to make apt and skilful use of words and expressions in various contexts, from narrowly defined technical or professional fields to the broadest social arenas. Each of these different contexts, broad or narrow, constitutes a different language game, in which a specific set of rules applies; these rules are not right or wrong but may be more or less appropriate to a particular function or purpose in life.

the condensed idea
Language games

33 Science and pseudoscience

Fossils are the remains or traces of creatures that lived in the past, which turned to stone after their death and have been preserved within rocks. Tens of thousands of different kinds of fossils have been discovered …

1. … *ranging from primitive bacteria that lived and died 3.5 billion years ago to early humans, who first appeared in Africa within the last 200,000 years. Fossils and their arrangement within successive layers of rock are a treasure trove of information on the development of life on Earth, showing how later forms of life evolved from earlier ones.*

2. … *ranging from simple bacteria to early humans. All these extinct creatures, together with those that are alive today, were created by God in a period of six days about 6,000 years ago. Most of the fossilized animals died in a catastrophic global flood that occurred about 1,000 years later.*

Two dramatically opposed views on how fossils came into being and what they tell us. The former is a fairly orthodox view that might be given by a geologist or palaeontologist. The latter might be presented by a New Earth creationist, who holds that the account of the creation of the universe given in the Book of Genesis is literally true. Neither has much sympathy for the other's way of looking at things: the creationist believes that the orthodox scientist is radically mistaken in many crucial respects, most notably in accepting the theory of evolution by natural selection; the orthodox scientist thinks that the creationist is driven by religious zeal, perhaps politically motivated, and certainly deluded if they think they are engaged in a serious scientific enterprise. For creationism, according to the mainstream scientific view, is nonsense dressed up as science – or 'pseudoscience'.

Science matters

What precisely is science? Clearly we need an answer to that question if we are to tell impostors from the real thing. In any case the question

The sequential chronology underlying evolution requires that there are never any geological 'reversals' (fossils turning up in the wrong rock strata). This is an entirely testable and readily falsifiable hypothesis: we only need to find a single dinosaur fossil in the same rock as a human fossil or artefact and evolution is blown clean out of the water. In fact, amongst all the millions of fossil specimens that have been unearthed, not a single reversal has ever been found: massive confirmation of the theory. For the creationist, this same evidence is enormously awkward. Amongst the many desperate attempts to explain away the evidence, one suggestion is a 'hydraulic sorting action', in which different body density, shape, size, etc. are supposed to cause differential rates of sinking and hence to sort animals into different layers. Another idea is that the smarter animals were better able to escape to higher ground and hence avoid drowning for longer. If you are in a geological hole ...

matters – the pretensions of science are enormous and can scarcely be exaggerated. Human life has been transformed beyond recognition in the space of just a few hundred years: devastating diseases have been eradicated; journeys that would have taken weeks can be completed in hours; humans have landed on the Moon; the subatomic structure of matter has been revealed. These and a myriad other astonishing achievements are credited to science. The transformative power of science is so vast that merely the claim that something is 'scientific' is often intended to discourage critical analysis or appraisal. But not all the developments of mainstream science are beyond criticism, while some claims from the fringes of science – or from pseudoscience beyond them – can be meretricious, self-serving or downright dangerous. So the ability to recognize the real thing is crucial.

The hypothetical method

The usual conception is that the 'scientific method' is hypothetical: it starts from data obtained by observation and other means and then moves to theory, attempting to frame hypotheses that explain the data in question. A successful hypothesis is one that stands up to further testing and generates predictions that would not otherwise have been anticipated. The movement is thus from empirical observation to generalization, and if the generalization is good and survives prolonged examination, it may eventually be accepted as a universal 'law of nature' that is expected to hold true in similar circumstances, irrespective of time and place. The difficulty for this conception of science, recognized over 250 years ago by David Hume, is the so-called 'problem of induction' (see page 109).

Underdetermination of theory by evidence

Another way of making essentially the same point is to say that a scientific theory is always 'underdetermined' by the available evidence:

Falsification

An important response to the problem of induction was given by the Austrian-born philosopher Karl Popper. In essence he accepted that the problem could not be resolved but chose to sidestep it. Instead, he suggested no theory should ever be considered proved, no matter how much evidence there is to support it; rather, we accept a theory until it has been falsified (or disproved). So while a million and one observations of white sheep cannot *confirm* the general hypothesis that all sheep are white, a single observation of a black sheep is sufficient to falsify it.

Falsifiability was also, in Popper's view, the criterion by which to distinguish true science from its imitators. A 'contentful' scientific theory takes risks, making bold predictions that can be tested and shown to be wrong; a pseudo-science, by contrast, plays safe and keeps things vague in the hope of evading exposure. Falsificationism is still influential today, though many would not accept its exclusion of induction from scientific methodology or the rather simplistic relationship it assumes between scientific theories and the (supposedly neutral or objective) evidence on which they are based.

the evidence alone is never sufficient to allow us to definitively choose one theory over another. Indeed, in principle any number of alternative theories can always be made to explain or 'fit' a given set of data. The question then is whether the various qualifications and *ad hoc* additions needed in order to shore up a theory are more than it can stand. This process of adjustment and refinement is a proper part of the methodology of science, but if the weight of evidence counting against a theory is too great, there may be no (rational) alternative but to reject it.

The problem for creationism is that there is a veritable tsunami of evidence counting against it. To take just two examples:

- the radiometric and other dating methods that underpin geology, anthropology and planetary science have to be completely discarded in order to accommodate a New Earth chronology;

- the stratified arrangement of fossils within rocks and the spectacular absence of reversals (the wrong fossils appearing in the wrong places) – all compelling evidence for evolution – require extravagant contortions from the creationist.

Creationism also introduces a whole raft of problems of its own. For instance, a massive water source would be required to achieve a global inundation, and no suggestion to date (icy comet strike, vapour canopy over the atmosphere, subterranean deposit, and so on.) has been remotely plausible. It is often said against creationism is that it doesn't take risks – it doesn't make the bold and falsifiable claims characteristic of true science. It would perhaps be fairer to say that it makes some fantastically risky claims that are unsupported by evidence of any kind.

the condensed idea
Evidence falsifying hypotheses

34 Paradigm shifts

'**I**f I have seen a little further it is by standing on the shoulders of Giants.' Isaac Newton's famous comment to fellow scientist Robert Hooke neatly captures a popular view of the advance of science. Scientific progress is a cumulative process, it is supposed, in which each generation of scientists builds on the discoveries of its predecessors: a collaborative march – gradual, methodical, unstoppable – towards a greater understanding of the natural laws that govern the universe.

A popular and attractive picture, perhaps, but seriously misleading according to the American philosopher and historian Thomas S. Kuhn. In his highly influential 1962 book *The Structure of Scientific Revolutions*, Kuhn gives a much bumpier, jumpier account of scientific development: a history of fitful and intermittent progress punctuated by revolutionary crises known as 'paradigm shifts'.

Normal and revolutionary science

In a period of so-called 'normal science', according to Kuhn, a community of like-minded scientific workers operate within a conceptual framework or world-view called a 'paradigm'. A paradigm is an extensive and flexibly defined assemblage of shared ideas and assumptions: common methods and practices, implicit guidelines on suitable topics for research and experimentation, proven techniques and agreed standards of evidence, largely unquestioned interpretations passed from generation to generation, and more. Scientists working within a paradigm are not concerned to venture outside it or to blaze new trails; instead, they are mainly engaged in resolving puzzles thrown up by the conceptual scheme, ironing out anomalies as they arise, and gradually extending and securing the boundaries of the domain.

A period of normal science may continue for many generations, perhaps for several centuries, but eventually the efforts of those within the community create a mass of problems and anomalies that begin to undermine and challenge the existing paradigm. This finally sparks a crisis that encourages some to look beyond the established framework and to begin devising a new paradigm, whereupon there is a shift or

Scientific truth and scientific relativism

A central feature of Kuhn's picture of scientific change is that it is culturally embedded in a whole host of historical and other factors. Though Kuhn himself was keen to distance himself from a relativistic reading of his work, such an account of how science develops casts doubt on the very notion of scientific truth and the idea that the aim of science is to discover objectively true facts about how things are in the world. For what sense does it make to talk of objective truth when each scientific community sets its own goals and standards of evidence and proof; filters everything through a web of existing assumptions and beliefs; makes its own decisions about which questions to ask and what counts as a good answer? The usual view is that the truth of a scientific theory is a matter of how well it stands up alongside neutral and objective observations about the world. But as Kuhn and others have shown, there are no 'neutral' facts; there is no neat line between theory and data; every observation is 'theory-laden' – covered in a thick mulch of existing belief and theory.

migration of workers – which may take years or decades – from the old paradigm to the new. Kuhn's own favoured example was the traumatic transition from the Ptolemaic Earth centred world-view to the heliocentric system of Copernicus. Another seismic paradigm shift was the supplanting of Newtonian mechanics by quantum physics and relativistic mechanics in the early 20th century.

The exaggerated discontinuities and dislocations supposed by Kuhn's account have meant that it has remained contentious as a historical thesis, but it has nevertheless proved highly influential among philosophers of science. Of particular interest has been the claim that different paradigms are 'incommensurable' – that basic differences in their underlying logic mean that results achieved in one paradigm are effectively incompatible with, or untestable within, another paradigm. For example, while we might expect that the 'atoms' of the Greek philosopher Democritus cannot be compared with those split by Ernest Rutherford, incommensurability suggests

Rutherford's atoms are different again from the ones described by modern quantum mechanics. This logical discontinuity within the grand architecture of science ran directly counter to the view that had prevailed before Kuhn's time. Previously it had been accepted that the edifice of scientific knowledge was built up steadily and rationally on foundations laid by earlier workers. At a stroke, Kuhn had swept away the idea of concerted progress towards a single scientific truth and put in its place a landscape of diverse, locally determined and often conflicting scientific aims and methods.

The disunity of science

It has long been assumed that science is an essentially unified endeavour. It has seemed reasonable to talk of a 'scientific method' – a single, well-defined set of procedures and practices that could in principle be applied to many different scientific disciplines; and to speculate on the prospect of some kind of grand unification of the sciences, in which all laws and principles would somehow collapse into an overarching, exhaustive and internally consistent structure. The key to such a coming-together is supposedly a fully reductive account of the sciences, the usual suggestion being that everything will ultimately be subsumed under physics. Recent work, however, has brought a fuller appreciation of the cultural and social embeddedness of the sciences and a greater emphasis on the essential disunity of science. And with it has come a realization that the search for a single scientific method is probably chimerical.

the condensed idea
Science – evolution and revolution

35 Occam's razor

Crop circles are geometrical patterns of flattened wheat, barley, rye, and so on. Such formations, often extensive and highly intricate in design, have been found throughout the world in ever-increasing numbers since the 1970s. Much reported in the media, there was at first feverish speculation over their origin.

Among the favoured theories were that:

1. the circles marked the landing sites of alien spaceships, or UFOs, which had left the distinctive patterns on the ground;

2. the circles had been created by human hoaxers, who had come at night, equipped with ropes and various other tools, to create the marks and so stoke up media attention and speculation.

Both explanations appear to fit the available evidence, so how do we decide which of these or the other available theories we should believe? In the absence of any other information, can we make a rational choice of one theory over its rivals? According to a principle known as Occam's razor, we can: where two or more hypotheses are offered to explain a given phenomenon, it is reasonable to accept the simplest one – the one that makes fewest unsupported assumptions. Theory 1 assumes that UFOs exist, an assumption for which there is no clear supporting evidence. Theory 2 makes no assumptions about paranormal activity; indeed it assumes only the kind of prankish human behaviour that has been common throughout history. So we are rationally justified – provisionally and always allowing that new evidence may become available – in believing that crop circles are the work of human hoaxers.

In fact, in this case Occam's razor is spot on. It is now known that theory 2 is correct, because the hoaxers concerned have admitted as much. Is the razor always as reliable as this?

Ambitions and limitations

Sometimes known as the principle of parsimony, Occam's razor is in essence an injunction not to seek a more complicated explanation for something where a simpler one is available. If several alternative explanations are on offer, you should (other things being equal) favour the simplest. Occam's razor is sometimes criticized for not doing what it does not in fact set out to do. Empirical theories are always 'underdetermined' by the data on which they are based (see page 134), so there are always several possible explanations for a given body of evidence. The principle does not claim that a simpler explanation is correct, merely that it is more *likely* to be true and so should be preferred until there are grounds for adopting a more elaborate alternative. It is essentially a rule of thumb or methodological injunction, especially valuable (one would suppose) in directing one's efforts in the early stages of an investigation.

The razor in action

Although generally not explicitly credited, Occam's razor is frequently wielded in scientific and other rational debates, including many that appear in this book. The brain in a vat problem (see page 4) sets up two rival scenarios, both apparently compatible with the available evidence: we are real physical beings in a real world, or we are brains in vats. Is it rational to believe the former rather than the latter? Yes, according to Occam's razor, because the former is much *simpler*: a single real world, rather than the virtual world created by the vat, plus the vat apparatus, evil scientists and so on. But here, as often elsewhere, the problem is shifted, not solved: for how do we tell which scenario is simpler? You could, for instance, insist that the number of physical objects is what matters and therefore that a virtual world is simpler than a real one.

In a similar vein, the other minds problem (see page 44) – the problem of how we know that other people have minds – is sometimes dismissed with a flourish of the razor: all sorts of other explanations are possible, but it is rational to believe that people have minds like our own because attributing conscious thoughts to them is much the *simplest* explanation of their behaviour. Again, though, the razor is seriously blunted by questions over what counts as simple.

The razor is often used against a range of dualist accounts, on the grounds that it is simpler not to introduce another layer of reality, level of explanation, and so on. Unnecessary complexity – positing separate mental and physical realms and then struggling to explain how they are connected – lies at the heart of many objections to Cartesian mind–body dualism. The razor may slice away one layer of reality, but it doesn't of course indicate which one to throw away. Today physicalists – those who suppose that everything (including us) is ultimately open to physical explanation – form the great majority, but there will always be some like George Berkeley who take the other, idealist path (see page 15).

A blunt razor?

The idea of simplicity can be interpreted in different ways. Is the injunction against introducing unwarranted entities or unwarranted hypotheses? These are very different things: keeping the number and complexity of hypotheses to a minimum is sometimes referred to as 'elegance'; minimizing the number and complexity of entities as 'parsimony'. And they can run counter to each other: introducing an otherwise unknown entity, such as a planet or a subatomic particle, might allow a great deal of theoretical scaffolding to be dismantled. But if there is such a basic uncertainty about the meaning of the razor, is it reasonable to expect any firm guidance from it?

the condensed idea
Keep it simple

36 What is art?

'I have seen, and heard, much of Cockney impudence before now; but never expected to hear a coxcomb ask two hundred guineas for flinging a pot of paint in the public's face.' So, infamously, the Victorian critic John Ruskin expressed his condemnation of James McNeill Whistler's phantasmagorical *Nocturne in Black and Gold* of 1875. The libel action that ensued led to an apparently nominal victory for the artist – he was awarded damages of just one farthing – but in reality it gave him much more: a platform from which to plead the rights of artists to express themselves, unfettered by critical constraints, and to raise the war cry of aestheticism – 'art for art's sake'.

Ruskin's utter incomprehension of Whistler's work is nothing unusual. Each successive age sees a restaging of the battle between artist and critic, in which the latter – often mirroring conservative public taste – cries out in horror and disdain at the supposed excesses of a new and assertive generation of artists. In our own time we witness the constant wringing of critical hands at the latest artistic atrocity: a pickled shark, a urine-soaked canvas, an unmade bed. The conflict is timeless and beyond resolution because it is motivated by a fundamental disagreement on the most basic of questions: what is art?

From representation to abstraction

Ruskin and Whistler's conceptions of the properties that a work of art must have share little common ground. In philosophical jargon, they disagree on the nature of aesthetic value, the analysis of which constitutes the central question in the area of philosophy known as aesthetics.

The view among the Greeks was that art is a representation or mirror of nature. For Plato, ultimate reality resided in a realm of perfect and unchanging Ideas or Forms – inextricably associated with the concepts of goodness and beauty (see page 8). He regarded works of art as a mere reflection or poor imitation of these, inferior and unreliable as a path to truth; so he dismissed poets and other artists from his ideal republic. Aristotle shared the conception of art as representation but took a more sympathetic view of its objects, regarding them as a completion of what was only partially realized in nature, so offering insight into the universal essence of things.

The idea of art as representation and its close association with beauty held sway well into the modern period. In reaction to this, a number of 20th-century thinkers proposed a 'formalist' approach to art, in which line, colour and other formal qualities were regarded as paramount and all other considerations, including representational aspects, were downplayed or excluded. Thus form was elevated over content, paving the way for the abstractionism that came to play a more dominant role in Western art. In another influential departure from representation, expressionism renounced anything resembling close observation of the external world in favour of exaggeration and distortion, using bold unnatural colours to express the inner feelings of the artist. Instinctive and consciously non-naturalistic, such

The eye of the beholder

At once the most basic and the most natural question in aesthetics is whether beauty (or any other aesthetic value) is really 'in', or inherent in, the objects to which it is ascribed. Realists (or objectivists) hold that beauty is a real property that an object may possess and that its doing so is entirely independent of anyone's beliefs about it or responses to it; Michelangelo's *David* would be beautiful even if no human existed to judge it so (even if everyone thought it ugly). An anti-realist (or subjectivist) believes that aesthetic value is necessarily tied to the judgements and responses humans make. As in the parallel question of whether moral value is objective or subjective (see page 52), the sheer oddness of beauty being 'out there in the world' independent of human observers may force us to an anti-realist position – to believe that beauty is indeed in the eye of the beholder. Nevertheless, our intuitions strongly support the feeling that there is *something* more to an object being beautiful than the mere fact of our finding it to be so.

Some support for these intuitions is given by Kant's idea of universal validity: aesthetic judgements are indeed based purely on our subjective responses and feelings; yet such responses and feelings are so ingrained in human nature that they are universally valid – we can reasonably expect any properly constituted human to share them.

expressions of the artist's subjective emotion and experience were regarded as the hallmark of true works of art.

Family resemblance

A perennial theme of Western philosophy since Plato has been the pursuit of definitions. The Socratic dialogues typically pose a question – what is justice, what is knowledge, what is beauty – and then proceed to show, through a series of questions and answers, that the interlocutors do not in fact have a clear understanding of the concepts involved. The tacit assumption is that true knowledge of something depends on being able to define it, and it is this that those debating with Socrates are unable to do. But this presents us with a paradox, for those who cannot provide a definition of a given concept are generally able to recognize what it *isn't*, which surely requires that they must know, at some level, what it *is*.

The concept of art confronts us with just such a case. We seem to know what it is, yet struggle to define the necessary and sufficient

---

The institutional theory

'They were asking me questions like: *"Is it art?"* And I was saying *"Well, if it isn't art ... what the hell is it doing in an art gallery and why are people coming to look at it?"* '

This remark by the British artist Tracey Emin echoes the 'institutional theory' of art, widely discussed since the 1970s. This theory holds that works of art qualify as such purely by virtue of having the title bestowed on them by authorized members of the art world (critics, those responsible for galleries, artists themselves, and so on). While influential, the institutional theory is beset by difficulties, not least that it is highly uninformative. We want to know *why* works of art are considered valuable. Members of the art world must have *reasons* for making the judgements they do. If they don't, what interest is there in their opinions? If they do, we should be much better informed by knowing them.

conditions for something to count as a work of art. In our perplexity, it is perhaps natural to ask whether the task of definition is not itself misconceived: a wild-goose chase whose aim is to pin down something that stoutly refuses to cooperate.

One way out of this maze is provided by Wittgenstein's notion of family resemblance, which he explains in his posthumously published *Philosophical Investigations*. Take the word 'game'. We all have a clear idea what games are: we can give examples, make comparisons between different games, arbitrate on borderline cases, and so on. But troubles arise when we attempt to dig deeper and look for some essential meaning or definition that encompasses every instance. For there is no such common denominator: there are lots of things that games have in common, but there is no single feature that they all share. In short, there is no hidden depth or essential meaning: our understanding of the word is no more or less than our capacity to use it appropriately in a wide range of contexts.

If we suppose that 'art', like 'game', is a family-resemblance word, most of our difficulties evaporate. Works of art have many things in common with other works of art: they may express an artist's inner emotions; they may distil the essence of nature; they may move, frighten or shock us. But if we cast around for some feature that they all possess, we will search in vain; any attempt to *define* art – to pin down a term that is essentially fluid and dynamic in its use – is misconceived and doomed to failure.

the condensed idea
Aesthetic values

37 The intentional fallacy

Many consider Richard Wagner to be among the greatest composers ever to have lived. His creative genius is scarcely in doubt; the constant procession of pilgrims to his 'shrine' in Bayreuth bears witness to his enormous talent and enduring appeal. Also beyond serious dispute is that Wagner was an exceptionally unpleasant man: staggeringly arrogant and self-obsessed, quite without scruple in exploiting others, disloyal to those closest to him … an endless catalogue of foibles and vices. And if anything, his views were even more repellent than his personality: intolerant, racist, virulently anti-semitic; a keen advocate of racial cleansing who called for the expulsion of Jews from Germany.

How much does any of this matter? Does our knowledge of Wagner's character, dispositions, beliefs, and so on, have any relevance to our understanding and appreciation of his music? We might suppose that such considerations are relevant to the extent that they inform or affect his musical works; that knowing what motivated him to produce a particular work or what intentions lay behind its creation could lead us to a fuller understanding of its purpose and meaning. However, according to an influential critical theory developed in the middle years of the 20th century, interpretation of a work should focus purely on its objective qualities; we should strictly disregard all external or extrinsic factors (biographical, historical, and so on) concerning the author of the work. The (alleged) mistake of supposing that the meaning and value of a work can be determined by such factors is called the 'intentional fallacy'.

Public works

Although the idea has since been introduced into other areas, the original provenance of the intentional fallacy was literary criticism. The term was first used in a 1946 essay by William Wimsatt and Monroe Beardsley, two members of the school of New Criticism that emerged in the USA in the 1930s. The main concern of the New Critics was that poems and other texts should be treated as independent and self-sufficient; their meaning should be determined purely on the basis of the words themselves – the author's intentions, stated or supposed, were irrelevant to the process of interpretation. A work, once released to the world, became a public object to which no one, including the author, had privileged access.

Drawing attention to the intentional fallacy was not purely a theoretical matter: it was intended as a corrective to prevailing trends in literary criticism. Certainly, as far as ordinary 'uncorrected' readers are concerned, it is clear that we do in fact depend on all sorts of extraneous factors in interpreting a text; it simply seems implausible to suppose that our reading of a book on the slave trade would be unaffected by knowing whether the author was African or European. It is of course another question whether it *should* have any such effect, but we ought perhaps to be wary of ideas that push us so far from common practice. It is indeed questionable whether it is even possible, let alone desirable, to make so complete a separation between an author's mind and its products. Making sense of a person's actions necessarily involves making assumptions about their underlying intentions; might not interpretation of a work of art depend in part on making similar assumptions and inferences? In the end it is hard to swallow the idea that what an author or artist intended a work to mean is actually *irrelevant* to what it really means.

Can immoral art be good?

A long-running debate in philosophy has centred around the question of whether art that is morally bad can itself be good (as art). The question has tended to focus on figures such as Leni Riefenstahl, the German film-maker whose documentaries *Triumph of the Will* (about the Nuremberg rallies) and *Olympia* (about the 1936 Berlin Olympics) were essentially Nazi propaganda but which are nevertheless considered by many to be technically and artistically brilliant. The ancient Greeks would have readily dismissed the question, as for them the notions of beauty and moral goodness were inextricably linked, but it has proved more troublesome for moderns. Artists themselves tend to be relatively indulgent, amongst whom the poet Ezra Pound is fairly typical: 'Good art however "immoral" is wholly a thing of virtue. Good art cannot be immoral. By good art I mean art that bears true witness.'

The dangers of the intentional fallacy warn us to ignore the creator's intentions when it comes to assessing the value and meaning of a work of art. But if we are forced to regard a putative work of art in isolation, cut off from the intentions of its maker, we may struggle to retain some distinctions we would be sorry (or at least surprised) to lose.

Suppose a forger creates a perfect Picasso – exactly in the style of the master, faultless down to the last brushstroke, undetectable as a fake by the experts. Normally we would downgrade a copy, however good, as it is not the work of the master; it is a slavish imitation, lacking originality and creative genius. But once the work is severed from its roots, aren't such considerations all so much hot air? A cynic might say that hot air is putting it mildly: preferring an original to a perfect copy is an unedifying mix of snobbishness, greed and fetishism. The intentional fallacy is an antidote to this, a reminder of the true value of art.

And what if there are no intentions to ignore – because there is no creator? Suppose that millions of chance lappings of the sea happen to shape a piece of wood into a beautiful sculpture, perfect in colour, texture, balance, and so on. We might treasure such a piece, but would it be a work of art – or art at all? It seems clear that it is not an artefact. So what is it? And what value does it have? The fact that it is not the product of human creativity changes the way that we look at it. But isn't this wrong, if the origins of the sculpture are irrelevant?

Finally, suppose that the greatest artist of the day carefully selects and displays a bucket and mop in a leading gallery. Then the cleaner comes along and happens to put down his or her identical bucket and mop alongside the 'work of art'. The artistic value, in this case, lies precisely in the process of selection and display. Nothing else separates the two buckets and mops. But if we consider only the objective character of the buckets and mops, is there really any difference? These thoughts suggest that we may need to reassess our attitudes towards art. There is a real danger of being dazzled by the emperor's new clothes.

The affective fallacy

In appreciating a text or a work of art – especially a complex, abstract or otherwise challenging one – we expect that different audiences will respond in different ways and form different opinions. We expect each interpreter to form their own interpretation, and in a sense each such interpretation imposes a different meaning on the work. On the face of it, the fact that these various meanings cannot all have been intended by the author or artist seems to support the idea of the intentional fallacy. However, in their unerring focus on the words themselves, the New Critics were no less concerned to exclude the reactions and responses of the reader in the evaluation of a literary work. The mistake of confusing the impact that a work might have on its audience with its meaning they called the 'affective fallacy'. Given the countless different subjective responses that different people might experience, it does seem unhelpful to tie these too closely to the meaning of the work. But, again, might not our evaluation of the supposedly objective qualities of a work be influenced by its capacity to elicit various responses from its audience?

the condensed idea
Meanings in art

38 The argument from design

'**L**ook round the world: contemplate the whole and every part of it. You will find it to be nothing but one great machine, subdivided into an infinite number of lesser machines, which again admit of subdivisions to a degree beyond what human senses and faculties can trace and explain. All these various machines, and even their most minute parts, are adjusted to each other with an accuracy which ravishes into admiration all men who have ever contemplated them. The curious adapting of means to ends, throughout all nature, resembles exactly, though it much exceeds, the productions of human contrivance; of human designs, thought, wisdom, and intelligence …

… Since, therefore, the effects resemble each other, we are led to infer, by all the rules of analogy, that the causes also resemble; and that the Author of Nature is somewhat similar to the mind of man, though possessed of much larger faculties, proportioned to the grandeur of the work which he has executed. By this argument a posteriori, and by this argument alone, do we prove at once the existence of a Deity, and his similarity to human mind and intelligence.'

This succinct statement of the argument from design for the existence of God is put into the mouth of its advocate Cleanthes by David Hume in his *Dialogues Concerning Natural Religion*, published posthumously in 1779. Hume's purpose is to set up the argument in order to knock it down again – and most consider that he did a very effective demolition job. It is a testament, however, to the argument's great stamina and intuitive appeal that it not only survived Hume's broadside but that it continues to resurface in modified guises to this day. While the argument was perhaps at the peak of its influence in the 18th century, its origins can be traced back to antiquity and it has never really fallen out of fashion since.

How the argument works

The abiding strength of the design argument rests on the powerful and widely held intuition that the beauty, order, complexity and apparent purpose seen in the world around us cannot *simply* be the products

The argument from design is also known as the 'teleological argument'. This is derived from the Greek word *telos*, meaning 'end' or 'purpose', because the basic idea underlying the argument is that the purpose we (apparently) detect in the workings of the natural world is evidence that there is a purposeful agent responsible for it.

of random and mindless natural processes. There must, it is felt, be some agent with the inconceivably vast intellect and skill needed to plan and bring into being all the wonderful things of nature, so exquisitely designed and fashioned to fill their various roles. Take the human eye, for instance: it is so intricately crafted and astonishingly well fitted to its purpose, it must have been designed to be so.

Starting from some favoured list of examples of such remarkable (apparent) contrivance in nature, the argument usually proceeds by way of analogy with human artefacts that clearly demonstrate the mark of their makers. So, just as a watch, for instance, is artfully designed and constructed for a particular purpose and leads us to infer the existence of a watchmaker, so the countless tokens of apparent intention and purpose in the natural world lead us to conclude that here, too, there is a designer at work: an architect equal to the task of designing the wonders of the universe. And the only designer with powers equal to such a task is God.

Cracks in design

In spite of its perennial appeal, some very serious objections have been raised against the design argument, by Hume and others. The following are among the more damaging.

- An argument from analogy works by claiming that two things are sufficiently similar in certain known respects to justify supposing that they also resemble each other in other, unknown respects. Humans and chimpanzees are sufficiently similar in physiology and behaviour that we may suppose (though we can never know for certain) that they, like us, experience sensations such as pain.

The divine and blind watchmakers

In his *Natural Theology* of 1802 the theologian William Paley set forth one of the most famous expositions of the design argument. If you happened to find a watch on a heath, you would inevitably infer from the complexity and precision of its construction that it must have been the work of a watchmaker; in the same way, when you observe the wondrous contrivances of nature, you are obliged to conclude that they, too, must have a maker – God. Alluding to Paley's image, the British biologist Richard Dawkins describes the process of natural selection as the 'blind watchmaker', precisely because it blindly fashions the complex structures of nature, without any foresight, purpose or directedness.

The strength of an analogical argument depends on the degree of relevant similarity between the things being compared. But the points of similarity between human artefacts (for example, cameras) and natural objects (for example, mammalian eyes) are in fact relatively few, so any conclusions we reach by analogy between them are correspondingly weak.

- The design argument appears to be vulnerable to an infinite regress. If the wondrous beauty and organization of the universe demand a designer, how much more so do this universe of wonders *plus* the architect behind it all? If we need a designer, it looks like we need an überdesigner too, and then an über-überdesigner, and then … So, while the denial of a regress lies at the heart of the cosmological argument (see page 156), in the design argument the threat of a regress looks plain vicious.

- The design argument's principal recommendation is that it explains how such marvels of nature as the human eye come to exist and function so well. But it is exactly such marvels and their fitness for purpose that are explicable in terms of Darwin's theory of evolution by natural selection, without any supernatural intervention by an

Cosmic fine-tuning

Some modern variants of the design argument are based on the staggering improbability that all the conditions in the universe were exactly as they had to be in order that life could develop and flourish. If any of the many variables, such as the strength of gravity and the initial heat of the expanding universe, had been just slightly different, life would not have got going in the first place. In short, there seems to be evidence of fine-tuning of the cosmos, so precise that we must suppose that it was the work of an immensely powerful fine-tuner. But improbable things do happen. It is incredibly unlikely that you will win a major lottery, but it is possible; and if you did, you wouldn't presume that someone had rigged the result in your favour – you would put it down to extraordinary luck. It may well be unlikely that life evolved, but it is only because it did that we are here to remark on how unlikely it was – and to draw erroneous conclusions from the improbability of its doing so!

intelligent designer. The divine watchmaker has apparently lost her job to the blind watchmaker.

- Even allowing that the case for design has been made, there are limitations on how much has actually been conceded. Many of nature's 'artefacts' might suggest design by committee, so we might need a team of gods and we are certainly not limited to one. Almost every natural object, however awe-inspiring in general, is less than perfect in detail; are not flawed designs indicative of a flawed (non-omnipotent) designer? Generally, the amount of bad in the world and its objects casts doubt on the morals of their maker. And of course there is no compelling reason to suppose that the designer, however good a job she did, is still alive.

the condensed idea
The divine watchmaker

39 The cosmological argument

Question: *Why is there something rather than nothing?*
Answer: *God.*

Such are the beginning and end of the cosmological argument, and there isn't a great deal in between. This is one of the classic arguments for the existence of God, and at once one of the most influential and (some would say) most dubious arguments in the history of philosophy.

In fact the 'cosmological argument' is a type or family of arguments, rather than a single one, but all the variants are comparable in form and similarly motivated. They are all empirically grounded, based (in the most familiar version) on the seemingly unobjectionable observation that everything that exists is caused by something else (see box opposite). This something else is in turn caused by something else again, and so on and on and on. To avoid going back forever in an infinite regress, we must reach a cause that is not itself caused by something else: the first and uncaused (or self-caused) cause of everything, and this is God.

Why isn't there nothing?

Leaving aside for a moment consideration of its merits, it must be admitted that the cosmological argument is a response to perhaps the most natural, basic and profound question we could possibly ask: why does anything at all exist? There might have been nothing, but there is something. Why? Like the other classic arguments for God's existence, the cosmological argument has its roots in antiquity, and it is the basis for the first three of Aquinas's *Quinque Viae* (or *Five Ways*), a set of five arguments for the existence of God. A modern cosmologist answering the question 'Why does anything exist?' would doubtless refer you to the big bang, the cataclysmic explosion 13 or so billion years ago that gave birth to the universe – to energy and matter and even to time itself. But this does not help much – it merely obliges us to rephrase the question: what (or who) caused the big bang?

The main difference between the different versions of the cosmological argument lies in the particular kind of relation between things they focus on. The most familiar version, sometimes known as the first-cause argument, takes a causal relation ('everything is caused by something else'), but the relation can be one of dependence, contingence, explanation, or intelligibility. The sequence of such relations cannot be extended indefinitely, it is argued, and in order that the sequence can be terminated, the starting point (that is, God) must lack the various properties in question. So according to the argument, God must be uncaused (or self-caused); independent of all things; non-contingent (that is, necessarily existent – it could not have been that it did not exist); self-explanatory; and intelligible without reference to anything else. (For simplicity, in this article the argument is stated in terms of the causal relation only.)

Making something out of a pig's ear

The attraction of the cosmological argument is that it addresses a very good question. At least, what looks like a very good question, and certainly a very natural one: why do we (and the rest of the universe) exist? Does the cosmological argument provide a good answer? There are a number of reasons to doubt it.

- The plausible-looking premise on which the cosmological argument is based – that everything is caused by something else – is based on our experience of how things are in the universe. But the argument asks us to extend this idea to something that is, by definition, *outside* our experience, because it is outside the universe: namely, to whatever it was that brought the universe into existence. Certainly, our experience can throw no light at all on this, and it is not obvious that the concept is even coherent: the universe means everything that exists, and its beginning (if it had one) also marks the beginning of time.
- On the face of it, the main premise of the argument (everything is caused by something else) contradicts its conclusion (something

– God – has no cause). To avoid this, God must lie outside the scope of 'everything', which must mean something like 'all things *in nature*'. In other words, God must be supernatural. This may be a satisfactory result for those who already believe the conclusion that the argument is supposed to lead us to. For others – who are the ones that need convincing – it merely adds to the mystery and fuels the suspicion that the foundations of the argument are essentially incoherent or unintelligible.

- The argument depends on the notion that an infinite regression of causes is intolerable: the chain must end somewhere, and that somewhere is God, who is uncaused (or self-caused). But is the idea of an infinite chain, implying that the universe had no beginning, really any harder to stomach than a supernatural something lying outside time?

- Even if we allow that the chain of causes has to end somewhere, why can't the something that is uncaused or self-caused be the universe itself? If the idea of self-causation is accepted, God becomes redundant.

- The cosmological argument obliges us to confer on God a number of very peculiar properties: that it be uncaused (or self-caused), necessarily existent, and so on. These are in themselves highly problematic and hard to interpret. What the argument does *not* prove (even allowing that it proves anything at all) is that God possesses the various properties consistent with the usual theistic account: omnipotence, omniscience, universal benevolence, and so on. The God that emerges from the cosmological argument is a very strange and attenuated one.

So what *did* cause the universe?

The nub of the problem with the cosmological argument is that, if the answer to the question 'What caused the universe?' is X (God, for instance, or the big bang), it is always possible to say 'Yes, but what caused X?' And if the answer to that is Y, one can still ask 'What caused Y?' The only way to stop the question being pushed forever backwards is to insist that X (or Y or Z) is radically different in kind such that the question cannot be posed. And this requires that some pretty weird properties are ascribed to X. Those who are reluctant to accept this consequence may be happier to accept the implication of

The god of the gaps

Historically, a god or gods have often been invoked to explain phenomena of nature that lie beyond the grasp of human understanding and knowledge. So, for instance, at a time when the physical causes of meteorological events such as thunder and lightning were not understood, it was common to explain them in terms of divine action or displeasure.

As science has advanced and human understanding progressed, the tendency has been for such explanations to be discounted and displaced. Before Darwin proposed the evolution of species by natural selection, the 'god of the gaps' was brought in to explain the seemingly inexplicable order and design apparent in the natural world (see page 152). In the case of the cosmological argument, God has retreated to the furthest extremity of human understanding – to the birth of the universe and to the very beginning of time. In such a deep redoubt, God may be beyond the reach of scientific enquiry. But at what cost? The kingdom of heaven has shrunk indeed.

extending the causal chain indefinitely, namely that the universe has no beginning. Or they may take the view adopted by Bertrand Russell that the universe is ultimately unintelligible, a brute fact that we cannot coherently talk or argue about. An unsatisfactory answer, but no worse than the others that are available to this most intractable of questions.

the condensed idea
The first and uncaused cause

40 The ontological argument

Take a moment to bring before your mental taste buds the greatest imaginable cashew nut: plump, elegantly sickle-curved, tangily salted and, most important, the texture – crumbling to a delicious milky, mushy, molar-cloying paste. All the qualities that make a great cashew nut, each present to the perfect degree. Yum, yum. Clearly in your mind? Now the good news. There is such a nut: the exquisite cashew, embodying the highest degree of all nutty perfections, truly exists!

For what we have in mind is the greatest imaginable cashew nut. Now a nut that exists in reality is surely a greater nut than one that exists only in the mind. So if the nut we are thinking of existed *only* in our minds, we could think of a greater nut – namely, the one that existed in our minds *and* in reality. But if this were so, we could imagine a greater nut than the greatest imaginable nut: a contradiction. So the nut we have in mind – the greatest imaginable cashew – really exists: the unbeatable nut must exist, otherwise it wouldn't be unbeatable.

From nuts to God

What is good for cashews is good for God. Or so suggests St Anselm, the 11th-century theologian who made the classic statement of the ontological argument, one of the most influential arguments for the existence of God. Eschewing cashew nuts altogether, Anselm starts from the uncontroversial (to him) definition of God as a being 'greater than which nothing can be conceived'. Now we can readily conceive of God as such, so God must exist as an idea in our minds. But if it existed *only* in our minds, we could conceive of an even greater being – namely one that exists in our minds and in reality. So, at pain of contradiction, God must exist not only in our minds but also in reality.

In contrast to the empirical basis of the argument from design and the cosmological argument, the ontological argument sets out to prove, a priori and as a matter of logical necessity, that God's existence cannot be denied without contradiction – that the very idea of God implies its existence. Just as we know, by understanding the meaning of the concept involved, that a square has four sides; in the same way, Anselm argues, by understanding the concept of God, we know that God exists.

Ontological objections

Like the cosmological argument, the ontological argument is really a family of arguments sharing a single core idea. All are equally ambitious, purporting to prove God's existence as a matter of necessity, but do they work? The situation is complicated as different variants of the argument are open to different kinds of criticism. Even Anselm presented two distinct versions – within the same work. The version given above – Anselm's first formulation of the argument and its classic statement – is vulnerable to two related lines of attack.

Modal logic and possible worlds

Anselm's second statement of the ontological argument proceeds much as the first, except 'existence' is replaced by 'necessary existence': the idea that God cannot be conceived *not* to exist; that it is logically impossible that it should *not* exist.

Necessary existence has inspired a number of recent attempts (notably by Alvin Plantinga) to rework the ontological argument using modal logic, in which the ideas of possibility and necessity are analysed in terms of logically possible worlds. For instance, let us suppose that 'maximally great' means 'exists and is omnipotent (etc.) in all possible worlds'; and let us allow that it is at least possible that a maximally great being exists (i.e. there is a possible world in which such a being exists). But such a being existing in one possible world *entails* that it exists in all worlds, so it necessarily exists. Rather than accept this conclusion, we may question the concessions that got us there; in particular, that a maximally great being might exist *in any* possible world. But to deny this possibility is to say that a maximally great being is self-contradictory. So perhaps God, conceived as a maximally great being, doesn't make sense?

All versions of the ontological argument turn on the idea that it is possible for us to conceive of a being greater than which nothing can be conceived. If this is not, in fact, possible – if the concept of God turns out to be unintelligible or incoherent – the whole argument falls flat. If the argument is to prove the existence of God as traditionally conceived (omniscient, omnipotent, etc.), these qualities must be individually coherent and jointly compatible, and each must be present in God to the highest possible degree. It is far from clear that this is possible. An omnipotent god must, for instance, be able to create beings with freewill; an omniscient god excludes the possibility that such beings could exist. It looks like omniscience and omnipotence cannot be present at the same time in the same being – quite a headache for the traditional view of God. Similar concerns over whether the idea of God as traditionally conceived is coherent lie at the root of the problem of evil (see page 164).

One of Anselm's earliest critics was a contemporary named Gaunilo, a monk of the Abbey of Marmoutier in France. Gaunilo's concern was that an ontological-type argument could be used to prove that *anything* existed. His own example was a perfect island, but the argument works just as well for cashew nuts and indeed for non-existent things like mermaids or centaurs. Clearly if a form of argument can prove the existence of non-existent things, the argument is in deep trouble. To resist this line of attack, the defender of the ontological argument must explain why God is a special case – how it differs in relevant respects from cashews. Some insist that the qualities or 'perfections' in which God's greatness resides are literally perfectible (capable in principle of attaining a highest degree) in a way that the properties of a great cashew are not. If God is able to do all that can conceivably be done, it is omnipotent to a degree that could not logically be surpassed; whereas if a plump cashew is a great cashew, it is still always possible to conceive a plumper and hence greater one.

So the very idea of the greatest imaginable cashew – in contrast to God, the greatest imaginable being – is incoherent. The corollary to this is that, if Anselm's argument is to work, his concept of God must be formed entirely of such intrinsically perfectible qualities. Ironically the apparent incompatibility between these very same qualities threatens to render the concept of God itself incoherent, so undermining all versions of the ontological argument (see box).

Gaunilo's problem is with verbal trickery – he suspects that Anselm has in effect defined God into existence. A similar basic concern underlies Kant's famous attack on the argument, in his 1781 *Critique of Pure Reason*. His objection lies with the implication (explicit in Descartes's influential reformulation) that existence is a property or predicate that can be ascribed to something just like any other. Kant's point, fully vindicated by 20th-century logic (see page 112), is that to say that God exists is not to attribute the property of existence to it (on a par with properties such as omnipotence and omniscience), but to assert that there is in fact an instance of the concept that has those properties; and the truth of that assertion can never be determined a priori, without seeing how things actually stand in the world. In effect, existence is not a property but a precondition of having properties. Anselm and Descartes have both made a logical blunder, the oddity of which is clear if you consider a statement such as 'Cashews that exist are tastier than those that don't'. Anselm makes an illicit jump from a concept to the instantiation of that concept: first he assumes that existence is a property that something may or may not have; then he claims that having such a property is better than not having it; and finally he concludes that God, as the greatest imaginable being, must have it. But this whole neat edifice crumbles at once if existence is denied the status of predicate.

the condensed idea
The greatest imaginable being

41 The problem of evil

Famine, murder, earthquake, disease – millions of people's futures blighted, young lives needlessly snuffed out, children left orphaned and helpless, agonizing deaths of young and old alike. If you could click your fingers and stop this catalogue of misery, you would have to be a heartless monster not to do so. Yet there is supposed to be a being that *could* sweep it all aside in an instant, a being that is unlimited in its power, knowledge and moral excellence: God. Evil is everywhere, but how can it exist side by side with a god who has, by definition, the capacity to put an end to it? That thorny question is the core of the so-called 'problem of evil'.

The problem of evil is without doubt the severest challenge confronting those who would have us believe in God. Faced with some terrible calamity, the most natural question is 'How could God let it happen?' The difficulty in coming up with an answer may seriously test the faith of those afflicted.

Is God ignorant, impotent, malevolent or non-existent?

The problem arises as a direct consequence of the qualities that are attributed to God within the Judaeo-Christian tradition. These properties are essential to the standard conception of God, and none can be jettisoned or modified without doing devastating damage to that conception. According to the traditional theistic account:

1. God is omniscient: it knows everything that it is logically possible to know.
2. God is omnipotent: it is able to do anything that it is logically possible to do.
3. God is omnibenevolent: it is of universal goodwill and desires to do every good thing that can possibly be done.

With particular regard to the problem of evil, the following inferences can plausibly be drawn from these three basic properties:

4. If God is omniscient, it is fully aware of all the pain and suffering that occurs.
5. If God is omnipotent, it is able to prevent all pain and suffering.
6. If God is omnibenevolent, it wishes to prevent all pain and suffering.

If propositions 4 to 6 are true and if God (as defined by propositions 1 to 3) exists, it follows that there will be no pain and suffering in the world, because God will have followed its inclinations and prevented it. But there is – manifestly – pain and suffering in the world, so we must conclude either that God does not exist, or that it does not have one or more of the properties set out in propositions 1 to 3. In sum, the problem of evil appears to have the implication, extremely unpalatable for the theist, namely that God doesn't know what is going on, doesn't care, or can't do anything about it; or that it doesn't exist.

Dodging the bullet

Attempts to avoid this devastating conclusion involve undermining some stage of the above argument. Denying that there is ultimately any such thing as evil, as advocated by Christian Scientists, solves the problem at a stroke, but such a remedy is too hard for most to swallow. Abandoning any of the three basic properties ascribed to God (limiting its knowledge, power or moral excellence) is too damaging for most theists to accept, so the usual strategy is to try to explain how evil and God (with all its properties intact) can in fact coexist after all. Such attempts most often involve attacking proposition 6 by claiming that there are 'morally sufficient reasons' why God might not always choose to eliminate pain and suffering. And underlying this idea is

What is evil?

Although this issue is conventionally called 'the problem of evil', the term 'evil' is not entirely apt. In this context the word refers, very broadly, to all the bad things that happen to people which, at one extreme, are too trivial to qualify as evil as normally conceived. The pain and suffering in question are due to both human and natural causes. It is usual to talk of 'moral evil' to cover the suffering caused by the immoral actions of human beings (murder, lying, and so on); and 'natural evil' to cover suffering caused by factors outside human control (natural disasters such as earthquakes and diseases not brought on by human activity).

the further assumption that it is in some sense in our interests, in the long run, that God should make such a choice. In sum, the occurrence of evil in the world is, ultimately, good: things are better for us than they would have been if that evil had not occurred.

So exactly what greater goods are to be gained at the cost of human pain and suffering? Probably the most powerful riposte to the problem of evil is the so-called 'freewill defence', according to which suffering on earth is the price we pay – and a price worth paying – for our freedom to make genuine choices about our actions (see page 168). Another important idea is that true moral character and virtue are forged on the anvil of human suffering: it is only by overcoming adversity, helping the oppressed, opposing the tyrant, and so on, that the real worth of the saint or hero is able to shine forth. Attempts to evade the problem of evil tend to run into difficulties when they try to explain the arbitrary distribution and sheer scale of human suffering.

Two problems of evil

The problem of evil can take two quite distinct, though related, forms. In the logical version (roughly as presented in the first part of this chapter), the impossibility of evil and God coexisting is demonstrated by deductive argument: it is claimed that the character of God is inconsistent with the occurrence of evil, and hence that belief in God is actually irrational. The evidential version of the problem of evil is in effect an inversion of the design argument (see page 152), using the endless tale of horrors in the world to argue the improbability that it is the creation of an all-powerful, all-loving god. This second version is much less ambitious than the logical version, seeking only to urge that God is unlikely to exist, but it is harder to rebut as a result. The logical version is formally defeated by showing that the co-existence of God and evil is merely possible, however improbable this may be thought to be. The evidential version presents a greater challenge for the theist, who must explain how some higher good for humans emerges from the catalogue of evil in the world.

So often it is the blameless that suffer most while the vicious go unscathed; so often the amount of suffering is out of all proportion with what might reasonably be required for purposes of character-building. In the face of so much dreadful misery, the theist's last resort may be to plead that 'God moves in mysterious ways' – that it is impudent and presumptuous for feeble-minded humans to second-guess the purposes and intentions of an all-powerful, all-knowing god. This is in effect an appeal to faith – that it is unreasonable to invoke reason to explain the workings of the divine will – and as such is unlikely to carry weight with those who are not already persuaded.

the condensed idea
Why does God let bad things happen?

42 The freewill defence

The presence of evil in the world offers the most serious challenge to the idea that there is an all-powerful, all-knowing and all-loving god. But evil exists, say the theists, because we make our own choices. Human freewill is a divine gift of enormous value, but God could not have made this gift to us without the risk of our abusing it. So God cannot be held responsible for bad things happening, for they are our fault alone and should not be used to cast doubt on God's existence.

The manifest existence of evil – the daily drama of pain and suffering that surrounds us – suggests that, if there is a god at all, it is far removed from the perfect being described in the Judaeo-Christian tradition. Instead, we are more likely to suppose a being that is either unwilling or unable to prevent terrible things happening, and hence one that is scarcely deserving of our respect, let alone our worship.

Attempts to block this challenge need to show that there are in fact sufficient reasons why a morally perfect god might yet choose to allow evil to exist. Historically the most popular and influential suggestion is the so-called 'freewill defence'. Our freedom to make genuine choices allows us to live lives of real moral worth and to enter into a

In popular culture

In the 2002 movie *Minority Report*, Tom Cruise plays police chief John Anderton in the Washington DC division of 'pre-crime'. Anderton arrests murderers before they actually commit the offence, since it is believed their actions can be foreseen with absolute certainty. When Anderton himself is accused, he becomes a fugitive, unable to believe he is capable of killing. In the end, pre-crime is discredited and determinism along with it, leaving the viewers' faith in freewill intact.

deep relationship of love and trust with God. But we can misuse our freedom to make the wrong choices. It was a risk worth taking and a price worth paying, but God could not have eliminated the possibility of moral baseness without depriving us of a greater gift – the capacity for moral goodness. In spite of its longevity and perennial appeal, the freewill defence faces some formidable problems.

Natural evil

Perhaps the most obvious difficulty that confronts the freewill defence is the existence in the world of natural evil. Even if we accept that freewill is a possession so precious that it is worth the cost in moral evil – the bad and vicious things brought about when people use their freedom to make wrong choices – what possible sense can we make of natural evil? How would God have undermined or diminished our freewill in any way if it had suddenly wiped out the HIV virus, haemorrhoids, mosquitoes, flash floods and earthquakes? The seriousness of this difficulty is illustrated by some of the theistic responses to it: that natural disasters, diseases, pests and the like are (literally) the work of the devil and a host of other fallen angels and demons; or that such afflictions are God's 'just' punishment for Adam and Eve's original sin in the Garden of Eden. The latter remedy traces all natural evil to the first instance of moral evil and

Quantum theory to the rescue?

Most philosophers have found the idea of determinism hard to resist, so have either accepted that freewill is illusory or struggled valiantly to find some accommodation. At the same time the attempts of libertarians to explain how events might occur without cause, or indeterminately, have tended to look *ad hoc* or just plain odd. But is the libertarian helped out by quantum mechanics? According to this, events at the subatomic level are indeterminate – matters of pure chance that 'just happen'. Does this provide a way to dodge determinism? Not really. The essence of quantum indeterminacy is randomness, so the idea that our actions and choices are at some profound level random does nothing to salvage the notion of moral responsibility.

The problem of freewill involves reconciling the view we have of ourselves as free agents fully in control of our actions with the deterministic understanding of those actions (and everything else) suggested by science. Simply put, the idea of determinism is that every event has a prior cause; every state of the world is necessitated or determined by a previous state which is itself the effect of a sequence of still earlier states. But if all our actions and choices are determined in this way by a series of events that extend back indefinitely, to a time before we were even born, how can we possibly be seen as the true authors of those actions and choices? And how can we conceivably be held responsible for them?

The whole notion of our acting freely seems to be threatened by determinism, and with it our status as moral beings. It is a deeply significant matter that has elicited a very wide range of philosophical responses. Amongst these the following main strands can be picked out:

- **Hard determinists** hold that determinism is true and that it is incompatible with freewill. Our actions are causally determined and the idea that we are free, in the sense that we could have acted differently, is illusory. Moral censure and praise, as normally conceived, are inappropriate.

thereby seeks to exonerate God from any blame. This explanation appears unconvincing. Is it not a monstrous injustice of God to visit punishment on the great-(great-great ...) grandchildren of the original offenders? And how does it benefit those already judged by the actions of their (distant) forebears to be given freewill in the first place?

The difficulty of natural evil aside, the freewill defence inevitably runs into a major philosophical storm in the form of the problem of freewill itself. The defence assumes that our capacity to make choices is genuinely free in the fullest sense: when we decide to do something, our decision is not determined or caused by any factor external to us; the possibility of doing otherwise is really open to us. This so-called 'libertarian' account of freewill accords well with our everyday sense

- **Soft determinists** accept that determinism is true but deny that it is incompatible with freewill. The fact that we could have acted differently if we had chosen gives a satisfactory and sufficient notion of freedom of action. It is irrelevant that a choice is causally determined; the important point is that it is not coerced or contrary to our wishes. An action that is free in this sense is open to normal moral assessment.

- **Libertarians** agree that determinism is incompatible with freewill and therefore reject determinism. The soft determinist's claim that we could have acted differently if we had chosen is empty, because not making such a choice was itself causally determined (or would have been had determinism been true). The libertarian thus holds that human freewill is real and that our choices and actions are not determined. The problem for libertarians is to explain how an action can occur indeterminately – in particular, how an uncaused event can avoid being random, as randomness will be no less damaging to the idea of moral responsibility than determinism. The suspicion is that there is a deep hole at the core of libertarianism; that the libertarian has ditched other explanations of human action and merely painted a big black box in their place.

of what is happening when we act and make choices, but many philosophers feel that it is in fact impossible to sustain in the face of determinism (see box above). And of course, if the libertarian account that underlies the freewill defence is unsustainable, the defence itself immediately collapses with it.

the condensed idea
Freedom to do wrong

43 Faith and reason

In spite of some heroic recent attempts to revive them, most philosophers would agree that the traditional arguments for the existence of God are effectively beyond resuscitation. Most religious believers would, however, be untroubled by this conclusion. Their belief does not depend on such arguments and would certainly not be shaken by their refutation.

For them, the normal standards of rational discourse are inappropriate to religious matters. Abstract philosophical speculation and reasoning did not lead them to belief in the first place and it will not convince them to renounce it either. It is indeed arrogant, they would claim, to suppose that our intellectual efforts could make God's purposes transparent or comprehensible to us. Belief in God is, ultimately, a matter not of reason but of faith.

Faith may be blind, but it is not simply a matter of 'just believing'. Those who elevate faith above reason – so-called 'fideists' – hold that faith is an alternative path to truth and that, in the case of religious belief, it is the right route. A state of conviction, achieved ultimately through God's action on the soul, nevertheless demands a voluntary and deliberate act of will on the part of the faithful; faith requires a leap, but it is not a leap in the dark. Philosophers, in contrast, wish to make a rational assessment of possible arguments in support of religious belief; to sift and weigh the evidence and reach a conclusion on that basis. Fideist and philosopher seem to be engaged in radically different projects. With apparently little or no common ground, is there any prospect of agreement or accommodation?

The balance sheet of faith

In fideistic hands, the fact that religious belief cannot be adequately defended on rational grounds is turned into a positive recommendation. If a (fully) rational route were open, faith would not be needed, but as reason fails to provide a justification, faith steps in to fill the gap. The act of will necessary on the part of the believer adds moral merit to the acquisition of faith; and a devotion that does not question its object is revered, at least by those who share it, as simple and honest piety. Some of the attractions of faith

Abraham and Isaac

The unbridgeable gap between faith and reason is well illustrated
by the biblical story of Abraham and Isaac. Abraham is held up
as the archetypal and paradigmatic example of religious faith for
his unquestioning willingness to obey God's commands, even to
the extent of sacrificing his own son, Isaac. Removed from its
religious context and looked at in a rational way, however,
Abraham's behaviour appears deranged. Any alternative reading
of the situation was preferable to and more plausible than the
one he chose (am I mad/did I mishear/is God testing me/is that
the devil pretending to be God/can I have that in writing?), so
his behaviour is simply and irretrievably incomprehensible to the
rationally inclined non-believer.

are obvious enough: life has a clear-cut meaning, there is some solace
for life's tribulations, believers have the consolation of knowing that
something better awaits after death, and so on. Religious belief clearly
answers many basic, primordial needs and concerns in humans,
and many people are undeniably improved, even transformed by
adopting a religious way of life. At the same time the symbols and
embellishments of religion have provided almost limitless artistic
inspiration and cultural enrichment.

Many of the points that the fideist would put on the credit side for
faith are set down as debits by the atheistic philosopher. Amongst the
most precious principles of secular liberalism, memorably set forth
by J.S. Mill, is freedom of thought and expression, which sits very
uneasily with the habit of uncritical assent extolled in the pious
believer (see box on page 175). The unquestioning devotion valued by
the fideist can easily look to the non-believer like credulity and
superstition. Ready acceptance of authority can lead people to fall
under the influence of unscrupulous sects and cults, and this can
sometimes tip over into fanaticism and zealotry. Placing one's faith in
others is admirable provided that the others concerned are themselves
admirable. When reason is shut out, all manner of excesses may rush
in to take its place; and it is hard to deny that at certain times and in

Pascal's wager

Suppose we feel that the evidence for God's existence is simply inconclusive. What should we do? We can either believe in God or not. If we choose to believe and are right (that is, God does exist), we win eternal bliss; and if we are wrong, we lose little. On the other hand, if we choose not to believe and are right (that is, God doesn't exist), we don't lose anything but don't gain much either; but if we are wrong, our loss is colossal – at best we miss out on eternal bliss, at worst we suffer everlasting damnation. So much to gain, so little to lose: you'd be a mug not to bet on God existing.

This ingenious argument for believing in God, known as Pascal's wager, was set forth by Blaise Pascal in his *Pensées* of 1670: ingenious, perhaps, but flawed. An obvious problem is that the argument requires that we *decide* what to believe, which just isn't the way belief works. Even worse, though, is that the impetus behind making the wager in the first place is that we don't have enough information about God to go on; yet making the right wager depends on having detailed knowledge of God's likes and dislikes. So what happens if God isn't too bothered about being worshipped but greatly dislikes calculating types who take gambles purely on the basis of their own self-interest?

certain religions sense and sympathy have flown out of the window to be replaced by intolerance, bigotry, sexism and worse.

So the balance sheet is drawn up, with debits and credits on each side, and often the assets on one side appear as liabilities on the other. To the extent that different accounting methods are used, the accounts themselves are meaningless, and this is often the abiding impression left when believers and non-believers debate with one another. They generally speak at cross-purposes, fail to establish any common ground, and succeed in moving each other not one inch. Atheists prove to their own satisfaction that faith is irrational; the faithful regard such supposed proof as irrelevant and quite beside the point. In the end, faith is irrational or non-rational; it proudly and defiantly sets itself in opposition to reason and, in a sense, that is precisely its point.

the condensed idea
The leap of faith

44 Positive and negative freedom

Freedom is one of those things that just about everybody agrees on. It matters, is a good thing and is one of the most important political ideals – perhaps *the* most important. Freedom is also one of those things that just about everybody *dis*agrees about. How much should we have? Is restriction necessary for freedom to flourish? How can your freedom to do one thing be reconciled with my conflicting freedom to do something else?

Tricky enough already, discussion of freedom (or liberty) is hampered still further by basic disagreement over its very nature. There lurks a suspicion that 'it' may not really be an it at all – not only might the word 'freedom' have several shades of meaning but it may refer to a number of quite distinct, if related, concepts. For shedding light on this murky scene, we are indebted to the influential 20th-century philosopher, Isaiah Berlin. At the centre of his discussion of liberty lies a crucial distinction between positive and negative freedom.

Two concepts of liberty

George is sitting with a glass of brandy in front of him. No one is holding a gun to his head, telling him to drink. There is no coercion and no impediment – nothing forcing him to drink and nothing preventing his drinking. He is at liberty to do as he pleases. But George is an alcoholic. He knows it's bad for him – it might even kill him. He may lose his friends, family, children, job, dignity, self-respect ... but he can't help himself. He stretches out his trembling hand and lifts the glass to his lips.

Two very different kinds of freedom are at play here. We often think of freedom as the absence of external restriction or coercion: you are free so long as there is no obstacle preventing you from doing what you want. This is what Berlin calls 'negative freedom'; it is negative in that it is defined by what is absent – any form of constraint or outside interference. In this sense George the drinker is completely free. But George can't help himself. He is compelled to drink, even though he knows his interests would be better served by not doing so. He is not fully in control of himself and his destiny is not fully in his own hands. To the extent that he is driven to drink, he has no choice and is not free. What George lacks is what Berlin calls 'positive freedom' – positive in that it is defined by what needs to be present within an agent (self-control, autonomy, the capacity to act in accordance with what are rationally assessed to be one's best interests). In this sense George is clearly not free.

Negative freedom

We are free, in Berlin's negative sense, to the extent that nobody interferes with our ability to act as we please. But in exercising our liberty, we inevitably tread on each other's toes. By exercising my freedom to sing loudly in the bath, I deny you the freedom to enjoy a quiet evening. No one can enjoy unfettered freedom without encroaching on the freedom of others, so when people live together in societies, some degree of compromise is needed.

The position adopted by classical liberals is defined by the so-called 'harm principle'. Most famously enunciated by the Victorian philosopher J.S. Mill in his *On Liberty*, this stipulates that individuals should be permitted to act in any way that does not bring harm to others; only where such harm is done is society justified in imposing restrictions. In some such way we can define an area of private liberty that is sacrosanct and immune to outside interference and authority. In this space individuals are allowed to indulge their personal tastes and inclinations without hindrance; and in a political sense they are at liberty to exercise various inviolable rights or freedoms – of speech, association, conscience, and so on.

While the negative understanding of liberty espoused by liberals is generally dominant, in Western countries at least, many thorny issues remain. In particular, we may wonder whether the liberty enjoyed by one who has neither the ability nor the resources to do what he is 'free' to do really merits the name. This is the shadow of liberty that leaves any citizen of the USA free to become president. True, there is no legal or constitutional barrier, so all citizens are to that extent free to do so; but in fact many are effectively debarred because they lack the necessary resources, in terms of money, education and social status. In sum, they lack the *substantive* freedom to exercise the rights that they *formally* hold. But in remedying these deficiencies in order to transform merely formal freedom to real, substantive freedom, the socially minded liberal may be obliged to endorse forms of state intervention that appear to be more appropriate to the positive interpretation of liberty.

Positive freedom

While negative freedom is freedom *from* external interference, positive freedom is usually characterized as freedom to achieve certain ends; as a form of empowerment that allows an individual to fulfil her potential, to achieve a particular vision of self-realization, to reach a state of personal autonomy and self-mastery. In a broader political sense, freedom in this positive sense is seen as liberation from cultural and social pressures that would otherwise impede progress towards self-realization.

Whereas negative freedom is essentially interpersonal, existing as a relation between people, positive freedom, by contrast, is intrapersonal – something that develops and is nurtured within an individual. Just as within George the drinker there is a conflict between his more rational side and his baser appetites, so generally the positive concept

---

The abuse of freedom

'O liberty! what crimes are committed in thy name!' So exclaimed Madame Roland before her execution in 1793. But the atrocities and excesses of the French Revolution are just one example of the horrors that have been perpetrated in the name of liberty – specifically liberty of the positive kind. Isaiah Berlin's deep distrust of positive liberty was fuelled by the enormities of the 20th century, especially those of Stalin. The trouble stemmed from a belief – the vice of the social reformer – that there is a single right course for society, a single cure for its ills. Against this view, Berlin himself was a strong proponent of pluralism in human values. There is a plurality of goods, he argued, that are distinct and incompatible, and from which people must make radical choices. His liberal attachment to negative freedom was underpinned by his view that this kind of freedom fostered the most propititious environment in which people could control and give shape to their lives by making such choices.

---

of freedom presupposes a division of the self into higher and lower parts. The attainment of freedom is marked by the triumph of the (morally, rationally) preferable higher self.

It was in part due to this concept of a divided self, which Berlin felt was implicit in the positive understanding of liberty, that he was so wary of it. To return to George: the part of him that properly understands his best interests is assumed to be the higher, more rational self. If he is incapable himself of encouraging this part to prevail, perhaps he needs some outside help – from people who are wiser than he and better able to see how he should act. It is then a short step for us to feel justified in physically separating George and his bottle of brandy. And what goes for George goes for the state too, Berlin feared: marching beneath the banner of (positive) freedom, government turns to tyranny, setting a particular goal for society; prioritizing a certain way of life for its citizens; deciding what they should desire with no regard for their actual desires (see box).

the condensed idea
Divided liberties

45 The difference principle

The dynamics of human societies are enormously complex, but it is reasonable to suppose that, in general, just societies are more stable and longer-lasting than unjust ones. The members of a society must believe that it is, by and large, fair if they are to abide by the rules that hold it together and to maintain its institutions. So how should the burdens and benefits of a society be distributed amongst its members in such a way as to make it just?

We might suppose that the only truly fair distribution of society's goods is one that is equal across all its members. Equality can mean different things, however. Do we mean equality of outcome, such that everyone has an equal share of the wealth and benefits that society has to offer and everyone has to shoulder an equal share of the burdens? But some people's shoulders are broader and stronger than others, and society as a whole may profit from the greater efforts that some of its members are able to make. If people are willing to make more effort, is it not reasonable for them to take a larger share of the benefits? Otherwise, those with greater natural talents may not exploit their gifts to the full, and society as a whole may be the loser. So perhaps the important thing is equality of *opportunity*, such that everyone in society has the same opportunities to prosper, even if some people make more of them than others and accrue more of the benefits in doing so.

In his *A Theory of Justice*, published in 1971, the US philosopher John Rawls made a highly influential contribution to the debate over social justice and equality. At the core of his theory lies the so-called 'difference principle', according to which inequalities in society are justified only if they result in its worst-off members being better off than they would otherwise have been. Rawls's principle has generated a vast amount of criticism, positive and negative, and it has been invoked (not always in ways that Rawls himself would have welcomed) in support of ideological positions across the political spectrum.

Behind the veil of ignorance
Any conception of social justice comprises, implicitly at least, the notion of impartiality. Any suggestion that the principles and

structures on which a social system is based are skewed towards a particular group (a social class or caste, for instance, or a political party) automatically renders that system unjust. To capture this idea of impartiality and to ground his principles of justice on fairness, Rawls introduces a thought experiment which has its origins in the social-contract theories of Hobbes and Rousseau (see page 184). We are asked to imagine ourselves in what he calls the 'original position', in which all personal interests and allegiances are forgotten: 'no one knows his place in society, his class position or social status, nor does anyone know his fortune in the distribution of natural assets and abilities, his intelligence, strength, and the like.' Though we might seek to further our own interests, we do not know where our interests lie, so special pleading is ruled out. Ignorant of what role in society we will be given, we are obliged to play safe and to ensure that no one group is disadvantaged in order to give advantage to another.

Rawlsian versus utilitarian

Much of the dynamic of Rawlsian justice comes from its opposition to a classic utilitarian approach to the same issues (see page 69). From a utilitarian perspective, any amount of inequality is justified provided that it results in a net gain in utility (that is, happiness). So, for instance, the interests of the majority could be sacrificed in return for a massive gain for a minority; or a massive loss for a minority could be justified provided that it resulted in a sufficient gain for the majority. Both of these possibilities would be ruled out by Rawls's difference principle, which prohibits the interests of the worst off being sacrificed in this way.

Another important contrast is that utilitarians are impartial in considering everyone's interests; each is required in effect to pool their interests with those of others and seek whatever outcome results in the highest net gain in utility. Rawlsians, on the other hand, placed in the original position, are acting egotistically; it is self-interest combined with ignorance of their future place in society that leads to prudential assent to the difference principle.

Horse-and-sparrow economics

Rawls's difference principle stipulates equality unless inequality benefits all, and so does not allow the interests of one group to be subordinated to those of another. The principle does not, however, have anything to say about the relative gains of the various beneficiaries, so a very small improvement for the worst off would justify a huge windfall for those who already enjoy the lion's share of society's goods. This has allowed the principle to be invoked by some who are very far removed from Rawls's own essentially egalitarian position. Thus Rawlsian corroboration was sometimes sought for the so-called 'trickle-down economics' of the Reagan and Thatcher administrations of the 1980s, in which tax cuts for the wealthiest were claimed to lead to increased investment and economic growth, so allegedly improving the fortunes of the less advantaged. This claim was disparagingly described by the economist J.K. Galbraith as 'horse-and-sparrow economics': 'if you feed enough oats to the horse, some will pass through to feed the sparrows.'

Impartiality, then, in a paradox that is apparent only, is the rational and inevitable choice of self-interested agents in the original position. Social and economic structures and arrangements can only be said to be distinctively just, Rawls claims, if they were contracted into from behind this imaginary 'veil of ignorance'. Moreover, whatever would be agreed to in such circumstances is the only thing that could be agreed to by individuals acting rationally and prudentially. And the best and most prudent thing that the rational decision-maker can do, to safeguard her own future (unknown) interests, is to embrace the difference principle.

The corollary of the difference principle – the idea that inequalities are acceptable only if they benefit the worst off – is that under any other circumstances inequalities are unacceptable. In other words, conditions of equality should exist except where the difference principle indicates that an inequality is permissible. Thus, for instance, economic arrangements that greatly enhance the position of the better off but leave the standing of the worst off unchanged would not count as just. People may, by accident of birth, have greater natural talents than others, but they should enjoy some social or economic advantage on that account only if their doing so leads to an improvement in the condition of the worst off. In sum, inequality is just only if everyone profits by it; otherwise equality should prevail.

the condensed idea
Justice as fairness

46 Leviathan

'**D**uring the time men live without a common Power to keep them all in awe, they are in that condition which is called Warre; and such a warre, as is of every man, against every man ... In such condition, there is no place for Industry; because the fruit thereof is uncertain; and consequently no Culture of the Earth; no Navigation, nor use of the commodities that may be imported by Sea; no commodious Building; no Instruments of moving, and removing such things as require much force; no Knowledge of the face of the Earth; no account of Time; no Arts; no Letters; no Society; and which is worst of all, continuall feare, and danger of violent death; And the life of man, solitary, poore, nasty, brutish, and short.'

The most famous passage from a masterpiece of political philosophy, this dystopic vision of humankind is painted by the English philosopher Thomas Hobbes in his book *Leviathan*, published in 1651. Dejected in the immediate aftermath of the English Civil War, Hobbes presents a picture of humanity that is consistently pessimistic and bleak: a vision of humans, living in an imagined 'state of nature', who are isolated, self-interested individuals whose sole object is their own security and their own pleasure; who are constantly in competition and conflict with one another, concerned only to get their own retaliation in first; amongst whom no trust and hence no cooperation is possible. The question for Hobbes is how individuals mired in such wretched and relentless discord can ever extricate themselves. By what means can any form of society or political organization develop from such unpromising origins? His answer: 'a common Power to keep them all in awe'; the absolute power of the state, symbolically named 'Leviathan'.

'Covenants, without the Sword, are but Words'

It is, in Hobbes's view, everyone's natural instinct to look after their own interest, and it is in everyone's interest to cooperate: only in this way can they escape from a condition of war and a life that is 'solitary, poore, nasty, brutish, and short'. If this is so, why is it not a simple matter for people in the state of nature to agree to cooperate with one another? It is no simple matter because there is always a cost to pay in complying with a contract and always a gain to be had from not complying – in the short term, at least. But if self-interest and self-preservation are the only moral compass, how can you be sure that someone else will not pre-emptively seek an advantage by non-compliance? Indeed, surely it is certain that they will seek such an advantage, so the best you can do is to break the contract first? Of course, everyone else reasons in the same way, so there is no trust and hence no agreement. In Hobbes's state of nature, long-term interest is always sure to give way to short-term gain, leaving no way out of the cycle of distrust and violence.

'Covenants, without the Sword, are but Words', Hobbes concludes. What is needed is some form of external power or sanction that forces

The noble savage

Hobbes's bleak view of humans in the 'state of nature' (that is, unrestricted by social and legal conventions) is not shared by his French successor, Rousseau. Where Hobbes sees the power of the state as a necessary means of taming people's bestial nature, Rousseau considers that human vice and other ills are the product of society – that the 'noble savage', naturally innocent, contented in the 'sleep of reason' and living in sympathy with his fellow men, is corrupted by education and other social influences. This vision of lost innocence and non-intellectualized sentiment proved inspirational for the Romantic movement that swept across Europe towards the end of the 18th century. Rousseau himself, however, was under no illusion that a return to some former idyllic condition was possible: once the fall from innocence was complete, the kind of social constraints envisaged by Hobbes were bound to follow.

people to abide by the terms of a contract that benefits them all – provided that they all abide by it. People must willingly restrict their liberties for the sake of cooperation and peace, on condition that everyone else does likewise; they must 'conferre all their power and strength upon one Man, or upon one Assembly of men, that may reduce all their Wills, by plurality of voices, unto one Will'. In this way citizens agree to cede their sovereignty to the state, with absolute power to 'forme the wills of them all, to Peace at home, and mutuall ayd against their enemies abroad'.

Of beasts and monsters

Leviathan, often linked with Behemoth, is a fearsome mythical sea monster that appears in various creation stories in the Old Testament and elsewhere. The name is used by Hobbes to suggest the awesome power of the state – 'that great LEVIATHAN, or rather (to speake more reverently) … that Mortall God, to which wee owe under the Immortall God, our peace and defence'. In modern usage, the word is usually applied to the state, with the suggestion that it is appropriating power and authority beyond its proper scope.

the condensed idea
The social contract

47 The prisoner's dilemma

'**T**hat's the deal: own up yourself and testify against your mate – he'll go down for 10 years and you just walk away.' Gordon knew the police could send them down for one year anyway, just for carrying the knives; but they didn't have enough to pin the robbery on them. The catch was that he also knew they were cutting the same deal with Tony in the next cell – if they both confessed and incriminated each other, they would each get five years. If only he knew what Tony was going to do …

… Gordon is no fool, so he carefully weighs up his options. 'Suppose Tony keeps quiet; then my best move is to inform on him – he'll get 10 years and I'll go free. And suppose he points the finger at me: it's still best to confess, inform against him, and get five years – otherwise, if I keep quiet, it'll be me doing the 10-year stretch. So either way, whatever Tony does, my best move is to confess.' The problem for Gordon is that Tony is no fool either and reaches exactly the same conclusion. So they incriminate each other and both get five years. Yet if neither had said anything, they would only have got one year each …

So the two men make a rational decision, based on a calculation of their own interest, and yet the outcome is clearly not the best available for either of them. What went wrong?

Game theory

The story outlined above, known as the 'prisoner's dilemma', is probably the most celebrated of a number of scenarios studied in the field of game theory. The object of game theory is to analyse situations of this kind, where there is a clear conflict of interests, and to determine what might count as a rational strategy. Such a strategy, in this context, is one that aims to maximize one's own advantage and will involve either working with an opponent ('cooperation', in game-theory terms) or betraying him ('defection'). The assumption is, of course, that such analysis casts light on actual human behaviour – either explaining why people act as they do or prescribing how they ought to act.

In a game-theory analysis, the possible strategies open to Gordon and Tony can be presented in a 'payoff matrix', as follows:

The dilemma arises because each prisoner is only concerned about minimizing his own jail term. In order to achieve the best outcome for both individuals collectively (each serving one year), they should collaborate and agree to forego the best outcome for each of them individually (going free). In the classic prisoner's dilemma, such collaboration is not allowed, and in any case they would have no reason to trust each other not to renege on the agreement. So they adopt a strategy that precludes the best outcome collectively in order to avoid the worst outcome individually, and end up with a non-optimal outcome somewhere in the middle.

Real-world implications

The broad implications of the prisoner's dilemma are that selfish pursuit of one's own interest, even if rational in some sense, may not lead to the best outcome for oneself or others; and hence that collaboration (in certain circumstances, at least) is the best policy overall. How do we see the prisoner's dilemma playing out in the real world? The prisoner's dilemma has been especially influential in the social sciences, notably in economics and politics. It may, for instance, give insight into the decision-making and psychology that underlie escalations in arms procurement between rival nations. In such situations, it is clearly beneficial in principle for the

---

Zero sum

Game theory has proved such a fertile field that some of its terminology has become common currency. A 'zero-sum game', for instance – often used informally, especially in business contexts – is technically a game such as chess or poker, where the winnings on one side are exactly balanced by the losses on the other, so the sum of the two is zero. In contrast, the prisoner's dilemma is a 'non-zero-sum' game, where it is possible for both players to win – and for both to lose.

parties concerned to reach agreement on limiting the level of arms expenditure, but in practice they rarely do. According to the games-theory analysis, the failure to reach an agreement is due to fear of a big loss (military defeat) outweighing a relatively small win (lower military expenditure); the actual outcome – neither the best nor the worst available – is an arms race.

A very clear parallel with the prisoner's dilemma is seen in the system of plea bargaining that underpins some judicial systems (such as in the US) but is forbidden in others. The logic of the prisoner's dilemma suggests that the rational strategy of 'minimizing the maximum loss' – that is, agreeing to accept a lesser sentence or penalty for fear of receiving a greater one – may induce innocent parties to confess and testify against each other. In the worst case, it may lead to the guilty party readily confessing their guilt while the innocent one continues to plead their innocence, with the bizarre consequence that the innocent party receives the more severe penalty.

Chicken

Another game much studied by game theorists is 'chicken', which featured most memorably in the 1955 James Dean film *Rebel Without a Cause*. In the game, two players drive cars towards each other and the loser (or chicken) is the one who swerves out of the way. In this scenario, the price of cooperation (swerving and losing face) is so small relative to the price of defection (driving straight and crashing) that the rational move appears to be to cooperate. The danger comes when player A assumes that player B is similarly rational and will therefore swerve, thus allowing him (player A) to drive straight with impunity and win.

The danger inherent in chicken is obvious – double defection (both drive straight) means a certain crash. The parallels with various kinds of real-world brinkmanship (potentially most calamitous, nuclear brinkmanship) are equally clear.

The most famous game theorist today is Princeton's John Forbes Nash. His mathematical genius and triumph over mental illness, culminating in a Nobel Prize for economics in 1994, are the subject of the 2001 film *A Beautiful Mind*.

As a game theorist, Nash's best-known contribution is defining the eponymous 'Nash equilibrium' – a stable situation in a game in which no player has any incentive to change their strategy unless another player changes theirs. In the prisoner's dilemma, double defection (both players confess) represents the Nash equilibrium which, as we have seen, does not necessarily correspond to the optimal outcome for the players involved.

the condensed idea
Playing the game

48 Theories of punishment

The mark of a civilized society, many would say, is its capacity to defend the rights of its citizens: to protect them from arbitrary treatment and harm from the state or other individuals, to allow them full political expression and to guarantee freedom of speech and movement. So what possible business is it of such a society to deliberately inflict harm on its citizens, to exclude them from the political process, to restrict their liberty to move and speak freely? For this is the prerogative the state takes upon itself when it chooses to punish its citizens for breaching the rules that it has itself imposed upon them.

This apparent conflict between different functions of the state shapes the philosophical debate over the justification of punishment. As in discussion of other ethical issues, debate over the justification of punishment has tended to divide along consequentialist and deontological lines (see page 65): consequentialist theories stress the beneficial consequences that follow from punishing wrongdoers, while deontological theories insist that punishment is intrinsically good as an end in itself, irrespective of any other benefits it may bring.

'It's no more than they deserve'

The key idea behind theories that hold punishment is good in itself is retribution. A basic intuition underlying much of our moral thinking is that people should get what they deserve: just as they should benefit from behaving well, so they should suffer for behaving badly. The idea of retribution – that people should pay a price for their wrongdoing – sits comfortably with this. Sometimes a further idea is brought in – the notion that wrongdoing creates an imbalance and that the moral equilibrium is restored by the wrongdoer 'repaying his debt' to society; an offender is under an obligation to society not to break its rules, and by doing so incurs a penalty that must be paid. The financial metaphor can neatly be extended to demand a fair transaction – that the severity of the penalty should match the severity of the crime.

The idea that 'the punishment should fit the crime' gets support from the *lex talionis* (law of retaliation) of the Hebrew bible: 'an eye for an eye, a tooth for a tooth'. This implies that crime and punishment should be equivalent not only in severity but also in kind.

The 'problem of punishment' is usually taken to be its justification in terms of utilitarian considerations such as deterrence and protection of society and/or intrinsic factors such as retribution. But it may also involve questions that are either more specific or more general. At a specific level, we may ask whether the punishment of a *particular* individual is justified. Such a question does not call into doubt the general propriety of punishment and is not of exclusively or especially philosophical interest.

Alongside such questions there are also issues of responsibility. Was the accused responsible in the sense required by law for his actions? Or was he acting under duress, or in self-defence? Here, the question of responsibility leads us into some very thorny philosophical ground. At the most general level, the problem of freewill asks whether all our actions are predetermined: do we exercise freedom of choice in any of our actions and, if not, can we be held accountable for *anything* we do?

Defenders of the death penalty often plead that the only proper reparation for the taking of life is the loss of life; such people are less quick to propose that blackmailers should be blackmailed or that rapists should be raped. This biblical support for retributivist theories gets to the heart of the main problem facing them; for the *lex talionis* is the work of a 'vengeful God' and the challenge for the retributivist is to keep a respectable distance between retribution and revenge. The idea that some crime 'cries out' for punishment is sometimes dressed up as the notion that punishment expresses society's outrage at a particular act, but when retribution is thus stripped down to little more than an urge for vengeance, it scarcely appears adequate, on its own, as a justification for punishment.

A necessary evil

In stark contrast to retributivist positions, utilitarian or other consequentialist justifications of punishment typically not only deny

The death penalty

Debates over the death penalty are usually structured in a similar way to those over other kinds of punishment. Proponents of capital punishment often argue that it is right for the most serious crimes to be punished by the severest penalty, irrespective of any beneficial consequences that might follow; but the supposed benefits – chiefly deterrence and protection of the public – are often cited too. Opponents counter by pointing out that the deterrent value is doubtful at best, that life imprisonment affords equal protection to the public, and that the very institution of capital punishment debases society. The strongest argument against the death penalty – the certainty that innocent people have been and will continue to be executed – is hard to resist. Perhaps the best argument in favour is that death is preferable to or less cruel than a life behind bars, but that could only ever lead one to conclude that an offender should be given the choice whether to live or die.

that it is a good thing but regard it as positively bad. The pioneer of classical utilitarianism, Jeremy Bentham, thought punishment was a necessary evil: bad because it adds to the sum of human unhappiness; justified only in so far as the benefits it brings outweigh the unhappiness it causes. Nor is this a purely theoretical position, as the eminently practical 19th-century prison reformer Elizabeth Fry makes clear: 'Punishment is not for revenge, but to lessen crime and reform the criminal.'

Punishment's role in reducing crime is generally understood to take two main forms: incapacitation and deterrence. An executed murderer will certainly not reoffend, nor will one who is incarcerated. The degree of incapacitation – especially permanent incapacitation through capital punishment – may be open to debate, but the need for some measures of this kind, taken in the public interest, is hard to contest. The case for deterrence is less easily made. On the face of it, it seems perverse to say someone should be punished, not for the crime they have committed, but in order to deter others from offending in a similar way; and there are doubts over its practical usefulness, in that studies suggest it is mainly fear of capture that deters, rather than any punishment that may follow.

The other main strand in utilitarian thinking about punishment is reform or rehabilitation of the criminal. There is an obvious attraction, to the liberal-minded at least, in the idea of seeing punishment as a form of therapy whereby offenders are re-educated and reformed in such a way that they can become full and useful members of society. There are serious doubts, however, over the ability of penal systems – most current systems, at least – to achieve any such objective.

In practice it is easy to produce counterexamples that show the inadequacy of any particular utilitarian justification for punishment – to cite cases where an offender does not present a danger to the public or does not need reform, or whose punishment would not have any deterrent value. The usual approach, therefore, is to offer a bundle of possible benefits that punishment may bring, without suggesting that all of them apply in all cases. Even then we may feel that something is lacking from a purely utilitarian account and that some space needs to be allowed for retribution. Reflecting this feeling, several recent theories are essentially hybrid in nature, attempting to combine utilitarian and retributivist elements in an overall account of punishment. The main tasks may then be to set priorities in the various specified objectives and to highlight where these conflict with current policies and practices.

the condensed idea
Does the punishment fit the crime?

49 Lifeboat Earth

'**A**drift in a Moral Sea ... So here we sit, say 50 people in our lifeboat. To be generous, let us assume it has room for 10 more, making a total capacity of 60. Suppose the 50 of us in the lifeboat see 100 others swimming in the water outside, begging for admission to our boat or for handouts ...

... We have several options: we may be tempted to try to live by the Christian ideal of being "our brother's keeper", or by the Marxist ideal of "to each according to his needs". Since the needs of all in the water are the same, and since they can all be seen as "our brothers", we could take them all into our boat, making a total of 150 in a boat designed for 60. The boat swamps, everyone drowns. Complete justice, complete catastrophe ... Since the boat has an unused excess capacity of 10 more passengers, we could admit just 10 more to it. But which 10 do we let in? ... Suppose we decide to ... admit no more to the lifeboat. Our survival is then possible although we shall have to be constantly on guard against boarding parties.'

In a paper published in 1974 the US ecologist Garrett Hardin introduced the metaphor of Lifeboat Earth to make the case against rich Western countries helping out the poorer developing nations of the world. Tireless scourge of bleeding-heart liberals, Hardin argues that the well-meaning but misguided interventions of the West are damaging in the long run to both sides. Countries on the receiving end of foreign aid develop a culture of dependence and so fail to 'learn the hard way' the dangers of inadequate forward planning and unchecked population growth. At the same time, unrestricted immigration means that near-stagnant Western populations will rapidly become swamped by an unstoppable tide of economic refugees.

The blame for these ills Hardin lays at the door of conscience-stricken liberals, censuring in particular their encouragement of the 'tragedy of the commons', a process in which limited resources, idealistically regarded as the rightful property of all humans, fall under a kind of common ownership that inevitably leads to their over-exploitation and ruin (see box opposite).

Toughlove ethics

Hardin himself is unapologetic about promoting his 'toughlove' lifeboat ethics. Untroubled by conscience himself, his advice to guilt-stricken liberals is to 'get out and yield your place to others', thereby eliminating feelings of remorse that threaten to destabilize the boat. There is no point worrying about how we got here – 'we cannot remake the past'; and it is only by adopting his tough, uncompromising stance that we can safeguard the world (or our part of it, at least) for future generations.

The picture of the relationship between rich and poor countries is certainly not pretty: the former safely ensconced in their boats and splitting open the heads and cracking the knuckles of the latter with their oars as they attempt to climb on board. But Hardin's is not the

The tragedy of the commons

Hardin's recourse to the harsh ethics of the lifeboat was a direct response to the shortcomings he perceived in the cosier 'spaceship Earth' metaphor beloved of head-in-the-clouds environmentalists; according to this, we are all onboard spaceship Earth together, so it is our duty to ensure that we do not waste the ship's precious and limited resources. The problem comes when this picture bleeds into the liberal's cherished image of one big, happy crew all working together, encouraging the view that the world's resources should be held in common and that everyone must have a fair and equal share of them. A farmer who owns a piece of land will look after his property and ensure that it is not ruined by overgrazing, but if it becomes common ground open to all, there will not be the same concern to protect it. The temptations of short-term gain mean that voluntary restraint soon evaporates, and degradation and decline rapidly follow. This process – inevitable, in Hardin's view, in 'a crowded world of less than perfect human beings' – is what he calls the 'tragedy of the commons'. In just this way, when the Earth's resources, such as air, water and the fish of the oceans, are treated as commons, there is no proper stewardship of them and ruin is sure to follow.

only way of interpreting the metaphor. Is the lifeboat really in danger of sinking? What is its real capacity? Or is it rather a matter of the bloated fat cats budging up a bit and taking a cut in their rations?

Much of Hardin's argument rests on the assumption that the higher reproductive rates of poorer countries would persist even if they got a fairer deal; he does not allow that such rates may be a *response* to high infant mortality, low life expectancy, poor education, and so on. Stripped of Hardin's gloss, the liberal would say, we are left with a picture of gross and naked immorality – selfishness, complacency, lack of compassion …

Moral boundaries

Looked at in this light, the liberal's guilt does not seem so out of place. A liberal incumbent of the lifeboat would not dream of clubbing a fellow passenger over the head with an oar, so how can she contemplate doing such a thing (or even allowing such a thing to be done) to the hapless individuals in the water surrounding the boat? Indeed, assuming that there is in fact room onboard, is she not duty-bound to help them out of the water and share her rations?

The lifeboat scenario thus presents Western liberalism with a nasty challenge. One of the most basic requirements of social justice is that people are treated impartially; things that are beyond someone's control (accidental factors due to birth, for instance, gender, skin colour, and so on) should not be allowed to determine how that person is treated and morally evaluated. And yet one such factor – where one happened to be born – seems to play a very significant role in our moral lives, not only for Hardin's supporters but for most self-professed liberals as well. How can so much – indeed, any – moral weight be attached to something as arbitrary as national boundaries? Faced with this challenge, the liberal must either show why the demands of impartiality can be suspended or watered down when we consider parts of the world other than our own – why it is right for us to show moral preference for our own; or she must accept that there is some incoherence at the heart of current liberalism and that consistency demands that principles of morality and social justice are extended globally.

Recent theorists have attempted to tackle the issue in both these ways. Argument for partiality as an essential ingredient in liberal thinking, while useful in addressing global realities, is certain to diminish its scope and dignity. On the other hand, full-blown cosmopolitan liberalism, while laudable, demands a sea change in current practices and policies of international engagement and risks foundering against those same global realities. Either way, there is still much groundwork to be done in political philosophy in the area of global and international justice.

the condensed idea
Is there more room in the boat?

50 Just war

Concerning warfare, most theorists would sympathize with the sentiments of the poet Charles Sorley, writing in 1915, a few months before his death, aged 21, at the battle of Loos: 'There is no such thing as a just war. What we are doing is casting out Satan by Satan.' However, many would also agree that war is to be avoided if possible, but not at any cost. It may be the lesser of two evils; the motive may be so compelling, the cause so important, that recourse to arms is morally justified. In these circumstances, war can be just war.

The philosophical debate over the morality of war has a long history. In the West, questions originally raised in ancient Greece and Rome were picked up by the Christian Church. The conversion of the Roman empire to Christianity in the fourth century prompted Aquinas to for a compromise between the pacifist leanings of the early Church and the military needs of imperial rulers. Augustine developed the now-canonical distinction between *jus ad bellum* ('justice in the move to war', the conditions under which it is morally right to take up arms) and *jus in bello* ('justice in war', rules of conduct once fighting is underway). Debate in 'just war theory' is essentially structured around these two ideas.

Conditions for war

The main aims of just war theory are to identify a set of conditions under which it is morally defensible to resort to force of arms and to offer guidelines on the limits within which fighting is to be conducted. The principles relating to *jus ad bellum* have been much debated and amended over the centuries. Some are more controversial than others; predictably, in most cases the devil has been in the detail of interpretation. It is generally agreed that the various conditions are all necessary, and none sufficient, to justify a move to war. Something approaching consensus has been reached around the following set of conditions.

Just cause

The overriding yet most disputed condition for morally defensible war is just cause. In earlier centuries this was interpreted quite broadly and might include, for instance, some form of religious motivation;

in the secular West such a cause would now generally be discounted as ideological, hence inappropriate. Most modern theorists have narrowed the scope of this condition to defence against aggression. Least controversially, this would include self-defence against a violation of a country's basic rights – its political sovereignty and territorial integrity (for example, Kuwait against Iraq in 1990–1); and most would extend it to cover assisting a third party suffering such aggression (for example, the coalition forces liberating Kuwait in 1991). Much more controversial is pre-emptive military action against a potential aggressor, where definitive proof of intention is inevitably lacking. In such cases, it may be moot whether pre-emptive force is not itself aggression, and some argue that only actual aggression – after it has happened – can constitute just cause.

Right intention

Closely allied with just cause is right intention. It is not enough to have just cause; it is necessary that the aim and only aim of military action is to further that cause. Aquinas talks in this connection of the promotion of good and avoidance of evil, but the crucial point is simply that the sole motivation should be to right the wrong caused by the aggression that provided just cause. Just cause cannot be a fig leaf for ulterior motives, such as national interest, territorial expansion or aggrandisement. So, liberating Kuwait as a response to Iraqi aggression is justified; doing so with the ultimate objective of securing oil interests is not.

Proper authority

That a decision to take up arms can only be made by the 'proper authorities' following due process appears obvious. 'Proper' basically means whatever body or institution of the state holds sovereign power (its competence to declare war will generally be defined within the country's constitution). 'Declare war' is significant, as it is sometimes added that the intention to take up arms should be formally declared to a country's own citizens and to the enemy state(s). This, however, seems perverse if doing so confers any strategic advantage on the enemy, which has certainly forfeited any right to such consideration by initiating aggression. 'Proper authority' is itself an extremely knotty concept, raising tricky questions about legitimate government and the appropriate relationship between decision-makers and people.

Last resort

Resort to war is only justified if – however just the cause – every other peaceful, non-military option has been tried or at least considered. If, for instance, a conflict could be averted through diplomatic means, it would be categorically wrong to make a military response. Economic or other sanctions should be considered, weighing their impact on civilians against the probable impact of military action.

Prospect of success

Even if every other condition for military intervention is met, a country should only resort to war if it has a 'reasonable' chance of success. This stipulation sounds prudent enough: there is no point

Jus in bello

The other aspect of just war theory is *jus in bello* – what constitutes morally acceptable and proper conduct once the fighting starts. This has a very wide scope, extending from the behaviour of individual soldiers in their relation to both the enemy and civilians, all the way up to major strategic questions, such as use of weapons (nuclear, chemical, mines, cluster bombs, and so on). In this area, two considerations are taken as paramount. *Proportionality* requires that means and ends are well matched. To take the extreme case, almost everyone accepts that nuclear attack cannot be justified, however successful it might be in bringing about some military objective. *Discrimination* requires that combatants and non-combatants are strictly distinguished. For instance, it is not considered permissible to target civilians, even if it might help erode military morale.

Clearly it is possible for a just war to be fought unjustly, and an unjust war justly. In other words, the requirements of *jus ad bellum* and of *jus in bello* are distinct, and one set may be satisfied without the other. Many aspects of *jus in bello*, in particular, overlap with the subject matter of international law (such as the Hague rules and Geneva conventions), and infringements on both winning and losing sides should in principle be assessed as war crimes.

in wasting lives and resources in vain. However, how successful is successful? Is it actually *wrong* for a weaker power to take on a stronger aggressor, however much the odds are stacked against it? The strongly consequentialist flavour of this condition is offensive to many. Sometimes it is surely right to resist an aggressor – and immoral, even cowardly, not to – however futile the action appears.

Proportionality

A balance between the desired end and the likely consequences of getting there: the expected good (righting the wrong that constitutes the just cause) must be weighed against the anticipated damage (casualties, human suffering, and so on). So, military action must be expected to do more good than harm; the benefit must be worth the cost. This is another prudential, strongly consequentialist consideration – though in this case almost irresistible if (a huge 'if') the resultant good and harm can be defined and accurately measured. In this area when we come to consider proportionality between military means and ends, we begin to stray into the territory of *jus in bello* – proper conduct in war (see box opposite).

Not just just war

Among today's philosophers, just war theory is probably the area of most active debate, but it is not the only perspective. The two extreme views are realism and pacifism. Realists are sceptical about the whole project of applying ethical concepts to war (or any other aspect of foreign policy); international influence and national security are the key concerns – real global players play hard-ball, morality is for wimps. Pacifists, in total contrast, believe that morality must hold sway in international affairs. Unlike the advocate of just war, military action, for the pacifist, is never the right solution – there is always a better way.

the condensed idea
Fight the good fight

Glossary

Terms within explanations that are **emboldened** have separate glossary entries.

Absolutism In ethics, the view that certain actions are right or wrong under any circumstances or whatever the consequences.

Aesthetics The branch of philosophy concerned with the arts, including the nature and definition of works of art, the basis of aesthetic value, and the justification of artistic judgement and criticism.

Analogy A comparison of the respects in which two things resemble one another; an argument from (or by) analogy uses known similarities between things to argue for similarity in some unknown respect.

Analytic Describing a proposition that gives no more infor mation than is contained in the meaning of the terms involved; e.g. 'All stallions are male.' By contrast, a proposition that does provide significant information ('Stallions run faster than mares') is described as synthetic.

Anti-realism *see* Subjectivism

A posteriori *see under* A priori

A priori Describing a proposition that can be known to be true without recourse to the evidence of experience. By contrast, a proposition that requires such recourse is knowable a posteriori.

Consequentialism In ethics, the view that the rightness of actions should be assessed purely by reference to their effectiveness in bringing about certain desirable ends or states of affairs.

Contingent Describing something that happens to be true but might have been otherwise. By contrast, a necessary truth is one that could not have been otherwise; something that is true in any circumstances or in all possible worlds.

Deduction A form of inference in which the conclusion follows from (is entailed by) the premises; if the premises of a valid deductive argument are true, the conclusion is guaranteed to be true.

Deontology The view that certain actions are intrinsically right or wrong, irrespective of their consequences; particular emphasis is placed on the duties and intentions of moral agents.

Determinism The theory that every event has a prior cause, and hence that every state of the world is necessitated or determined by a previous state. The extent to which determinism undermines our freedom of action constitutes the problem of freewill.

Dualism In the philosophy of mind, the view that mind (or soul) and matter (or body) are distinct. Substance dualists hold that mind and matter are two essentially different substances; property dualists hold that a person has two essentially different types of property, mental and physical. Opposed to dualism are idealism or immaterialism (minds and ideas are all there is) and physicalism or materialism (bodies and matter are all there is).

Empirical Describing a concept or belief that is based on experience (i.e. sense data or the evidence of the senses); an empirical truth is one that can be confirmed as such only by appeal to experience.

Empiricism The view that all knowledge is based on, or inextricably tied to, experience derived from the senses; the denial of a priori knowledge.

Epistemology The theory of knowledge, including its basis and justification and the role of reason and/or experience in its acquisition.

Fallacy An error of reasoning. Formal fallacies, in which the fault is due to the logical structure of an argument, are usually distinguished from informal fallacies, which comprise the many other ways that reasoning can go astray.

Freewill *see under* Determinism

Idealism *see under* Dualism

Immaterialism *see under* Dualism

Induction A form of **inference** in which an empirical conclusion (a general law or principle) is drawn from empirical premises (particular observations of how things are in the world); the conclusion is only supported (never entailed) by the premises, so the premises may be true, yet the conclusion false.

Inference A process of reasoning that moves from premises to conclusion; the principal types of inference are **deduction** and **induction**. Distinguishing good and bad inferences is the aim of logic.

Libertarianism The view that **determinism** is false and that human choices and actions are genuinely free.

Logic *see under* Inference

Materialism *see under* Dualism

Metaphysics The branch of philosophy that deals with the nature or structure of reality, generally focusing on notions such as being, substance and causation.

Naturalism In ethics, the view that moral concepts can be explained or analysed purely in terms of 'facts of nature' that are in principle discoverable by science.

Necessary *see under* Contingent

Normative Relating to the norms (standards or principles) by which human conduct is judged or directed. The normative/descriptive distinction aligns with the distinction between values and facts.

Objectivism In ethics and aesthetics, the view that values and properties such as goodness and beauty are inherent in, or intrinsic to, objects and exist independently of human apprehension of them.

Paradox In logic, an argument in which apparently unobjectionable premises lead, by apparently sound reasoning, to an unacceptable or contradictory conclusion.

Physicalism *see under* Dualism

Rationalism The view that knowledge (or some knowledge) can be acquired other than through the use of the senses, by exercise of our unaided powers of reasoning.

Realism The view that ethical and aesthetic values, mathematical properties, etc. really exist 'out there' in the world, independently of our knowing or experiencing them.

Reductionism An approach to an issue or area of discourse which aims to explain or analyse it, fully and exhaustively, in other (usually simpler or more accessible) terms, e.g. mental phenomena in purely physical terms.

Relativism In ethics, the view that the rightness or wrongness of actions is determined by, or relative to, the culture and traditions of particular social groups or communities.

Scepticism A philosophical position in which our claims to knowledge in some or all areas of discourse are challenged.

Subjectivism (or Anti-realism) In ethics and aesthetics, the view that value is grounded not in external reality but in our beliefs about it or emotional responses to it.

Synthetic *see under* Analytic

Utilitarianism In ethics, a **consequentialist** system in which actions are judged right or wrong to the extent that they increase or decrease human well-being or 'utility'; utility is classically interpreted as human pleasure or happiness.

Index

Greenfinch
An imprint of Quercus Editions Ltd
Carmelite House
50 Victoria Embankment
London EC4Y 0DZ

An Hachette UK company

First published in 2007
This revised edition published in 2022
Copyright © 2007, 2014, 2022 Ben Dupré

A CIP catalogue record for this book is available from the British Library

ISBN 978 1 52942 510 9
e Book ISBN 978 1 52942 870 4

10 9 8 7 6 5 4

Printed and bound in Great Britain by Clays Ltd, Elcograf S.p.A.

Papers used by Greenfinch are from well-managed forests and other responsible sources.